THE OFFICIAL
MANCHESTER UNITED
ANNUAL *2003*

ADAM BOSTOCK
WITH SIMON DAVIES

First published in 2002

Copyright © 2002
Manchester United Plc
Text and design copyright
© 2002 Carlton Books Limited

Manufactured and Distributed by
Carlton Books Limited
20 Mortimer Street
London W1T 3JW

A CIP catalogue of this book is available from
the British Library.

ISBN 0 233 050264

Design: **Andy Jones**
Photography: **John and Matthew Peters,
  Manchester United FC**
Picture Research: **Mark Granville**
Project Editor: **Martin Corteel**
Project Art Direction: **Darren Jordan**
Production: **Lisa French**

Printed in Italy

Contents

Match Day at OLD

Five hours to kick-off

10 am – A police briefing takes place so all officers are aware of their duties for the day. The stadium forecourt begins to fill up as the morning progresses, with fans visiting the Megastore to make sure they're kitted out in the latest gear. At 10.30 am, Matt Proctor begins a long day of match coverage on United's own radio station, broadcasting locally on 1413AM. Matt presents interviews, features and, of course, commentary on the game up until the station goes off-air at 6.30 pm.

If you think all the players, officials and staff just turn up at the ground half an hour before kick-off, you should think again! For some people, the typical match day starts much earlier than that … and ends a long time after the final whistle. Here's a guide to what goes on, based on the traditional 3 pm kick-off.

Above: **Fans outside the impressive East Stand.**
Right: **The Megastore starts to fill up.**
Below: **Manchester United Radio presenter Matt Proctor prepares to go on air.**

Eight hours to kick-off

7 am – Keith Kent and his early-rising ground staff get to work on the pitch. After having lovingly prepared the playing surface over the last few days, their last minute duties include rolling the pitch and painting the markings on. This is vital, as we'd never know if the ball had crossed the line for yet another United goal! As the morning progresses, match day essentials – food, drinks and programmes – are delivered to Old Trafford for sale throughout the day. Around the country, a platoon of United fans are waking up and getting ready to make their pilgrimage to their Holy Land.

TRAFFORD

Three hours to kick-off

12 pm – The most important people begin to arrive at Old Trafford – the players! After parking near the "Tradesmen's Entrance" – on the corner of the West and South Stands – they head up to their private restaurant for a healthy pre-match meal. From there they move to the dressing room to pull on the famous red shirt. The referee also arrives at midday, as does stadium announcer Alan Keegan, who will later introduce the teams to the crowd.

Forty minutes to kick-off

2.20 pm – The United team and substitutes head out onto the pitch for the first time, to be put through their pre-match paces by coach Mike Phelan. The hundreds or thousands of home fans who take their seats early shout words of encouragement to their favourite players and try to spot the away team's danger-men as they too warm up for the big match.

Kick-off

3 pm – While the men in red do their stuff out on the pitch, the boys in blue – otherwise known as the police – keep an eye on the crowd by watching the monitors in the stadium control room. In the press box (top right) journalists from around the world – including the reporter for

Manchester United's website ManUtd.com – are working hard to keep their readers, listeners or viewers up to date with the score.

Half-time

3.45 pm – The manager delivers his most important speech of the week in the dressing room, while the fans fill up on snacks from the many kiosks dotted around the stadium. The ground staff leap into action, repairing any damage done to the pitch during the first 45 minutes. Meanwhile, a celebrity United fan makes the half-time lottery draw. Somebody in the stadium will win £2000!

Head groundsman Keith Kent checks over the pitch at half-time.

Full-time

4.45 pm – The stadium empties very quickly. More often than not the United fans are celebrating a victory as they head for the tram, train, bus, taxi or car to travel home. In the press box, the newspaper journalists finish their "first draft" match reports before attending the post-match press conference. Later, they'll complete their articles with quotes from Sir Alex Ferguson and the away team manager.

Fifteen minutes after full-time

5 pm – Old Trafford's clean-up operation gets into full swing, with armies of workers (above) picking up litter inside and outside the stadium. The players clean up too – they dive into a warm post-match bath or shower before making their way to their private lounge for a well-earned drink with friends and family. **Cheers!**

Season's

2001/02

It promised to be a sweet sixteenth season for Sir Alex Ferguson when he unveiled two major signings in the summer of 2001. It was also supposed to be his last season, but after a few months of watching the exciting new boys Ruud van Nistelrooy and Juan Sebastian Veron in action, the Boss changed his mind! How could he leave, just as his new-look team was beginning to blossom? The answer is he couldn't … and boy, are we glad about that!

August 2001

Losing the FA Charity Shield at the start of the season wasn't the end of the world. United seem to lose it every year, and then win the title, so nobody from Manchester really cried when Liverpool left Cardiff's Millennium Stadium with the Shield. The Scousers won the match 2–1 but so what? United's museum staff were still polishing the prize that really mattered, the 2000/01 Premiership trophy, back at Old Trafford.

And it was at Old Trafford where the title machine fired up again, for the start of the league campaign. Fulham were newly promoted and plucky enough to score after just four minutes, then go 2–1 up just after half-time. But then the Reds rallied as new man Ruud van Nistelrooy blasted two goals

Giggs bangs in a great goal at Blackburn.

past his Dutch pal Edwin van der Sar. It was a fantastic first game for the Premiership season, and a fab result – 3–2 to United!

Goal of the Month: Ryan Giggs v Blackburn Rovers. The Welsh wizard starts and finishes a raid into Rovers territory, taking Veron's precision pass into the area and then blasting the ball home. Get in there!

FA Premiership (Top six)	P	W	D	L	F	A	Pts
1. Everton	3	2	1	0	5	2	7
2. Leeds	3	2	1	0	4	1	7
3. Arsenal	3	2	0	1	9	2	6
4. Bolton	2	2	0	0	6	0	6
5. Manchester United	3	1	2	0	6	5	5
6. Chelsea	2	1	1	0	3	1	4

Review

The Reds had little time to catch their breath, for three days later they travelled up the road to face Blackburn Rovers – or the Old Trafford Old Boys Club, as they're sometimes known! In fact, all the goals were scored by players from United's famous Youth team of 1992 – Ryan Giggs and David Beckham for the Champions, Keith Gillespie and Beckham (yes, him again, an own goal!) for Rovers. **Final score: 2–2.**

United conceded another early goal away to Aston Villa. After just four minutes, Darius Vassell scored past United's new goalkeeper Roy Carroll. Fabien Barthez was injured and Jaap Stam was also missing – Fergie had sold him to Lazio! Stam had been a rock in the Treble season, but even legends have to leave. Peter Schmeichel left United in 1999, but now he was back to haunt them, saving their shots for Villa. He couldn't stop Alpay's own goal, though. **Final score: 1–1.**

September 2001

Ruud was on a roll, Beckham back in business ... then Veron shone in early September with an exquisite individual performance which had fans, pundits and fellow players drooling with delight.

Goal of the Month: Juan Sebastian Veron v Tottenham Hotspur. The fab number four fires in a left-foot shot following a one-two with Van Nistelrooy and good approach play by Beckham, Silvestre and Scholes.

FA Premiership (Top six)	P	W	D	L	F	A	Pts
1. Arsenal	7	4	2	1	16	5	14
2. Manchester United	7	4	2	1	22	13	14
3. Leeds	6	4	2	0	9	1	14
4. Bolton Wanderers	8	3	3	2	10	6	12
5. Sunderland	8	3	3	2	8	7	12
6. Newcastle United	6	3	2	1	11	9	11

Against Everton, the Argentine genius showed off his full range of passing from fancy flicks to forty-yard heat-seekers, and also rattled in his first goal in English football to put United 1–0 up. Just after half-time they were 3–0 up, thanks to first goals of the season from Andy Cole and Quinton Fortune. Kevin Campbell pulled one back but then Beckham, super-sub on the day, took his regular share of the glory. **Final score: 4–1 to the Reds.**

A similar match saw another team in blue leave Old Trafford *with* the blues – Ipswich Town. Like Everton, they conceded two in the first half (in this case to Ronny Johnsen

Below: Viva Veron! Seba celebrates his goal at Spurs, in front of the Spurs fans!

and Ole Gunnar Solskjaer) and two in the second (Solskjaer again, and Cole). Unlike Everton, the Tractor Boys never looked like digging up a goal. **Final score 4–0.**

If Ipswich and Everton at home were easy, Newcastle and Spurs away were anything but! Two of the best matches of the season saw fifteen goals scored at either end. At Newcastle, United went 1–0 down, then Ruud equalised. Then they went 3–1 down, but Giggs and Veron made it 3–3. Finally Shearer scored the late winner for Newcastle. **Final score: 3–4.**

For the Spurs match, see page 37.

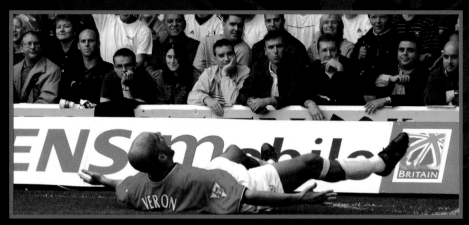

October 2001

How could United follow the thrilling 5-3 win at Spurs? By taking another three points home from their next trip, that's how, even though some of the top stars were taking a break. Ruud van Nistelrooy, Juan Sebastian Veron, Fabien Barthez and England's World Cup qualifying hero David Beckham all missed the match at Sunderland; luckily Andy Cole and Ryan Giggs didn't miss the target, and neither

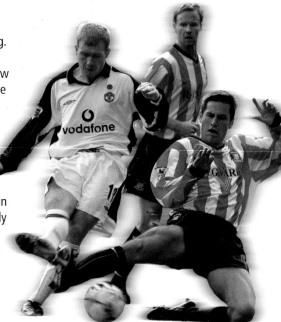

Barthez: flying saves, followed by silly errors.

Right: **Scholes on the ball against Sunderland.**
Above: **Stand-in captain Ryan celebrates his goal at Sunderland with Luke Chadwick.**

did poor Sunderland defender Stanislav Varga, whose own goal opened the scoring. Final score: 3–1 to United.

After winning two away matches in a row in the Premiership, Manchester United were hot favourites to win their next game at home. The visitors had other ideas though and, playing with all the gusto you'd expect in a derby match, Bolton Wanderers did what nobody expected them to do. They beat the Champions at Old Trafford. It had all been going to plan for United when Veron scored with a deadly free-kick but then Bolton bounced back through Kevin Nolan and Michael Ricketts. Final score: 1–2.

Nobody knew what to expect when Leeds United came to Old Trafford for the last Premiership match of October.

Goal of the Month: Ole Gunnar Solskjaer v Leeds. Veron's free-kick against Bolton was fabulous, but Ole's goal against Leeds was more important. The man from the Norwegian fishing town leaped like a salmon to head the ball in. Yessss!

FA Premiership (Top six)	P	W	D	L	F	A	Pts
1. Aston Villa	10	6	3	1	17	8	21
2. Leeds United	10	5	5	0	13	4	20
3. Arsenal	10	5	4	1	22	9	19
4. Liverpool	9	6	1	2	17	9	19
5. Manchester United	10	5	3	2	27	17	18
6. Newcastle United	10	5	2	3	18	14	17

At this stage of the season, the Champions were lethal in attack but loose in defence, sometimes in the same game. Against Leeds, they were neither. The Reds only conceded one goal, Mark Viduka's strike in the 77th minute, but they only scored one. Ole Gunnar Solskjaer's party-piece, an equaliser in the dying moments, saw relief erupt all around the ground as another dreaded defeat was avoided. Final score: 1–1.

Leicester's Walker (left) and Sinclair grimace as Ruud celebrates his goal.

November 2001

Solskjaer's salvation act only delayed defeat for another week. Losing to Leeds would have been bad, doing it to Liverpool was even worse. This time, there was far more at stake than the Charity Shield. Three league points were up for grabs and the Scousers snatched them all with three clinical goals scored by Michael Owen (2) and John-Arne Riise. All the goals, including David Beckham's consolation goal, were scored in a spell of twenty minutes, but United were just as poor in the other seventy.
Final score: 1–3.

United's critics blamed Barthez for the Liverpool result, and not for the last time. The word 'crisis' started to creep into newspaper articles about the club; some writers reckoned that selling Jaap Stam was the biggest mistake of all. Like a wounded lion, United wound themselves up for the next big game, and made easy meat of Leicester City. Van Nistelrooy scored, so did Yorke, and Barthez saved a re-taken penalty.
Final score: 2–0.

Just when the fans thought it was safe to think of the title again, United slipped up again to their biggest rivals. Arsenal had already beaten the Reds once in November but that was in the Worthington Cup, the day after the Liverpool game, and Fergie had fielded some fledglings. This time there were no such excuses, especially not for Fabien, who gifted two late goals to Henry and three points to Arsenal. A 1–1 draw, featuring goals by Scholes and Ljungberg, had suddenly been turned into a 3–1 defeat starring Barthez.
Final score: 1–3.

Captain for the day David Beckham looks bemused after losing to Liverpool.

Goal of the Month: Dwight Yorke v Leicester City. Not a lot to shout about in November… except for Yorkie's peach of a header. The Tobagan timed his run to perfection, to plant the ball home from Gary Neville's cross. Goaaaal!							
FA Premiership (Top six)	P	W	D	L	F	A	Pts
1. Liverpool	12	8	2	2	22	11	26
2. Leeds United	13	6	6	1	16	8	24
3. Arsenal	13	6	5	2	28	15	23
4. Newcastle United	13	7	2	4	23	17	23
5. Aston Villa	13	6	5	2	18	12	23
6. Manchester United	13	6	3	4	31	23	21

December 2001

Everybody could see why Sir Alex had tipped Chelsea as title challengers when they thrashed United 3–0 at Old Trafford! It was a fine performance by the Blues but it was the troubled Reds that really interested the critics. One pundit even spotted, quite cruelly, that the first letters of the teams that had beaten United in the league spelled out BLANC – Bolton, Liverpool, Arsenal, Newcastle and Chelsea!

The United fans remained faithful, of course, even standing to applaud their fallen heroes from the field at the end of

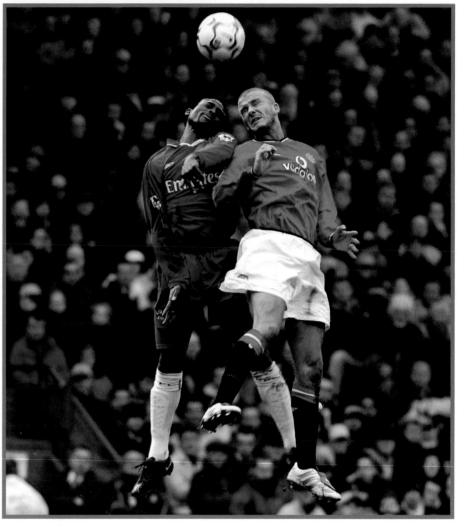

Becks and Babayaro battle for the ball during Chelsea's surprise victory.

Not a happy chappie! Ferguson's expression tells its own story as United lose 3–0 to Chelsea.

the Chelsea game, and again when United lost their next league match at home, 0–1 to West Ham. The fans would very soon be rewarded for their loyalty and patience, as the Reds bounced back to enjoy their best Christmas for many years.

The next two home games could not have been more different! First, the Reds destroyed Derby County 5–0, then they slaughtered Southampton 6–1! In between, they managed to win 1–0 at Middlesbrough – all three of those games are featured in 'Six of the Best' on page 31.

The festive fun continued on Boxing Day, when United beat a poor Everton team 2–0 at Goodison Park, and on the day before New Year's Eve when Fulham were a handful, just as they had been on the opening day. Jean Tigana's team again scored twice past Barthez, but again lost 3–2. It was the Ryan and Ruud show that shot down the Craven Cottage men, Giggs scoring two and setting up the other for the flying Dutchman.

Goal of the Month: Phil Neville v Southampton. On a day when Ruud took home the matchball, Phil took the biscuit with the fantastic final goal. The right-back cut inside, drifting past a few defenders and then unleashing a tremendous 20-yarder that gave the keeper no chance of saving it. What a strike!

FA Premiership (Top six)	P	W	D	L	F	A	Pts
1. Arsenal	20	11	6	3	41	24	39
2. Newcastle United	20	12	3	5	38	25	39
3. Leeds United	20	10	8	2	30	17	38
4. Liverpool	19	11	4	4	29	19	37
5. Manchester United	20	11	3	6	48	30	36
6. Chelsea	20	8	9	3	31	16	33

Two-goal Scholes celebrates with Solskjaer, at home to Newcastle.

Unfortunately, like all good things, the winning run had to come to an end. Doubly unfortunate, it ended against Liverpool, Danny Murphy's late goal making the final score 0–1 at Old Trafford. The score at Middlesbrough a few days later was even worse, 0–2, a defeat that dumped the Reds out of the FA Cup.

After a couple of blanks back-to-back, United needed to wrap up the month with some goals. Just a few days after their miserable trip to Middlesbrough, they bounced back at Bolton, winning 4–0. Van Nistelrooy scored yet again but this time Solskjaer stole the headlines, and the matchball, with a marvellous hat-trick.

January 2002

After a cracking Christmas, there was plenty to cheer in the New Year, starting with the Newcastle match at Old Trafford. The Magpies were among the league's high flyers but they had their wings clipped by one of Fergie's old fledglings, Paul Scholes. He scored two, and Ruud netted the other goal in an important 3–1 win.

Three seemed to be United's magic number. After beating Aston Villa 3–2 in the FA Cup (see 'Comeback Kings' on page 36) they won 3–1 at Southampton in the Premiership. The scorers were Beckham, Solskjaer and Van Nistelrooy, who was still on the same roll that included a hat-trick against the Saints in December. When Ruud equalised against them in United's win at St Mary's, it was the seventh league match in a row in which he had scored.

Seven equalled the Premiership record held by Thierry Henry and Alan Shearer – in the very next game, against Blackburn at Old Trafford, Ruud broke it (see 'Six of the Best' on page 31).

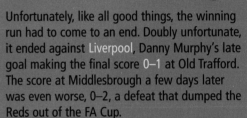

Goal of the Month: David Beckham v Southampton. There were a lot of goals to choose from but David's free-kick was both perfectly executed and perfectly timed, to put United 2-1 up just before the break. Nice one, Becks!

FA Premiership (Top six)	P	W	D	L	F	A	Pts
1. Manchester United	25	15	3	7	60	34	48
2. Arsenal	23	12	8	3	41	27	44
3. Newcastle United	23	13	4	6	42	29	43
4. Liverpool	24	12	7	5	33	24	43
5. Leeds United	23	11	9	3	35	21	42
6. Chelsea	23	9	10	4	40	23	37

David drives a deadly free-kick past Southampton keeper Paul Jones. What a cracker!

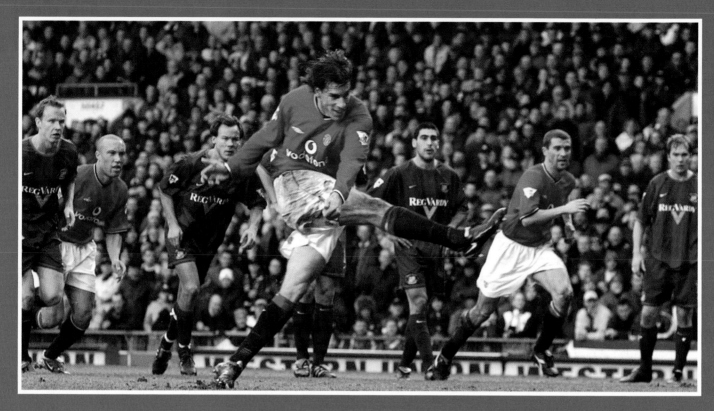

February 2002

United kicked off February with the same kind of flowing football and deadly finishing they had closed January with. What's more, they again scored four, for the second time in a week, as Sunderland were torn apart 4–1 at Old Trafford. All the best moments came in the first half, including Phil Neville's opening goal and Ruud van Nistelrooy's superb turn and volley. Even Sunderland's consolation goal, by Kevin Phillips, was a corker! Ruud's penalty on the brink of the break and another David Beckham free-kick completed the rout of Peter Reid's Black Cats.

The Reds were not only awesome at Old Trafford, they were also enjoying an excellent run on the road. Prior to visiting The Valley on 10 February, United had won five away matches in a row in the league. Ole Gunnar Solskjaer's two well-taken goals at Charlton Athletic, one in each half, made it six on the spin. **Final score: 2–0.**

Spinning was something that Ruud van Nistelrooy did time and again to shake off defenders in his debut season for the Reds. Another turn and shot on the newly laid Old Trafford turf took care of Aston Villa in late February, after Roy Keane had taken the ball away from George Boateng. Villa goalkeeper Peter Schmeichel had received a warm welcome on his return to the Theatre of Dreams but not even the great United legend could save Boateng from his nightmare moment. **Final score: 1–0 to the Champions.**

Ruud blasts in his penalty against Sunderland, to the delight of captain Keano.

Solskjaer's first goal against Charlton.

Goal of the Month: Ole Gunnar Solskjaer v Charlton Athletic. The first one, created by Roy Keane. The captain floated a fifty-yard pass to the Norwegian, who used great control to kill the ball with his first touch and then a killer instinct to fire past Dean Kiely from the left side of the box.

FA Premiership (Top six)	P	W	D	L	F	A	Pts
1. Manchester United	**28**	**18**	**3**	**7**	**67**	**35**	**57**
2. Arsenal	27	15	9	3	55	31	54
3. Liverpool	28	15	8	5	45	25	54
4. Newcastle United	26	16	4	6	51	33	52
5. Chelsea	26	11	11	4	46	26	44
6. Leeds United	26	11	10	5	37	29	43

March 2002

March can be make or break month in the race for the Championship. Fixtures come thick and fast, plenty of points are there to be won. Regrettably for Reds fans, United started March 2002 by dropping two points at Pride Park in Derby. Yes, the same team that had been turned over 5–0 at Old Trafford just before Christmas clawed their way back into the match to force a draw this time, 2–2. It was a bad result, especially after Paul Scholes and Juan Sebastian Veron had put the Reds in the driving seat at 2–1. However, it could have been worse. Malcolm Christie, who'd already scored two goals for Derby, thought he'd bagged the winner in the dying moments but it was rightly disallowed for a foul on Fabien. Phew!

United only had to wait three days to make amends, and they did so in style at home to Spurs, the team they had beaten 5–3 earlier in the season. This time, the Reds beat the men from North London 4–0. (For more details see 'Six of the Best' on page 31.)

If 5–3 at Spurs was the best away match of the season, then 5–3 at West Ham wasn't far behind it! The game played at Upton Park was pretty similar to the one at White Hart Lane. United struggled a bit in the first half, as if travelling down to London had taken its toll. But then after a few words of encouragement from the manager at half-time, the likes of Beckham, Butt, Scholes and Solskjaer really took control of the proceedings. All four of them scored from open play, Beckham also bagged a penalty. Great game!

If only United could have played away from home every week … they looked very lacklustre in their next match at Old Trafford, when they lost 0–1 to Middlesbrough. It was a poor performance by the Reds, and badly timed in a weekend when Liverpool beat Chelsea to go to the top of the table. Arsenal, meanwhile, were busy steaming their way into the FA Cup semi-finals by crushing Newcastle in the quarter-finals.

The pace in the three-horse title race didn't ease off on Easter Saturday, 30 March, when United, Arsenal and Liverpool all claimed victories. The Champions played first and thrilled the nation with their away win at Leeds. An early goal from Scholes and two in two minutes from Solskjaer made it 3–1 to United at half-time, and when Giggs grabbed the fourth, it should have been game, set and match. Leeds

The highs and lows of football – Becks trudges off the pitch after losing to Middlesbrough.

Becks slams home his second goal at Upton Park, from the penalty spot.

bounced back, though, from 4–1 to 4–3 to make the last ten minutes very tense indeed. Nail-biting stuff for Sir Alex!

Later on Easter Saturday, Arsenal won 3–0 at home to Sunderland, while Liverpool comfortably beat Charlton 2–0 at Anfield. Neither game was anywhere near as exciting as United's trip to Elland Road, but the results kept it very tight at the top of the table. What would happen in April was anybody's guess!

Goal of the Month: David Beckham v West Ham. The first one, delicately chipped from distance over the head of Hammers and England goalkeeper David James. Later described as "marvellous" by Sir Alex Ferguson.

FA Premiership (Top six)	P	W	D	L	F	A	Pts
1. Liverpool	32	19	8	5	53	26	65
2. Manchester United	**32**	**20**	**4**	**8**	**78**	**41**	**64**
3. Arsenal	30	18	9	3	60	32	63
4. Newcastle United	31	18	5	8	60	42	59
5. Leeds United	31	14	12	5	44	30	54
6. Chelsea	31	14	11	6	58	31	53

April 2002

United kept up their fantastic away form after Easter. They simply had to – all of their Premiership games in April were played away from home, and the Reds needed to win them all to keep up the pressure on Arsenal and Liverpool at the top of the table. The trip to Leicester looked like it might be a tricky one, especially without the injured Keano and Becks, but United rose to the challenge and sneaked a win with a goal by Ole Gunnar Solskjaer. **Final score: 1–0 to the Reds.**

Solskjaer struck again in the next away match, when United once more overcame what should have been a tough task. After all, Chelsea had won 3–0 at Old Trafford earlier in the season. Not only that, but the Blues were buzzing after reaching the FA Cup final. So it looked a tall order for Fergie's men to take three points from Stamford Bridge, but they did it with a polished, professional performance. Paul Scholes' thunderous shot and Ruud van Nistelrooy's tap-in put the Reds in the driving seat before half-time. Ole then wrapped up the perfect revenge result, scoring the third goal in United's superb win. **Final score: 3–0 to the Reds.**

The third and final Premiership match of April took the Reds on one of their longest journeys in the league, from Manchester to East Anglia. There they faced Ipswich Town, who were still scrapping to stay in the Premiership. Fight as they might, the Tractor Boys could do nothing about the bad luck that pushed them deeper into trouble. Chasing a ball into the area, van Nistelrooy tangled with a defender and fell to the ground – the referee awarded a penalty, and Ruud buried the ball into the net. **Final score: 1–0 to the Reds.**

One team's bad luck was another team's good luck, and United needed every bit of fortune they could get as they continued to chase Arsenal in the title race. They leapfrogged Liverpool, though, when the Scousers lost 1–0 at Spurs with only two matches left to play ...

Above right: **Scholes celebrates with Giggs after his sensational goal against Chelsea.**

Goal of the Month: Paul Scholes v Chelsea. Fifteen minutes into the match, Ryan Giggs lined up to take a free-kick on the right wing. But instead of curling a cross into the box or trying to shoot himself, he rolled the ball square to Scholes who blasted a thunderbolt past Carlo Cudicini. Fabulous goal!

Premiership (Top six)	P	W	D	L	F	A	Pts
1. Arsenal	36	24	9	3	74	33	81
2. Manchester United	36	24	4	8	87	44	76
3. Liverpool	36	22	8	6	58	27	74
4. Newcastle United	37	21	8	8	73	49	71
5. Leeds United	37	17	13	7	65	35	64
6. Chelsea	37	17	12	8	53	37	63

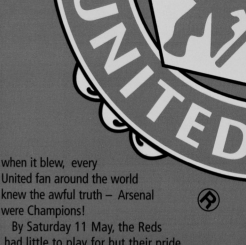

when it blew, every United fan around the world knew the awful truth – Arsenal were Champions!

By Saturday 11 May, the Reds had little to play for but their pride. Liverpool had climbed back into second place by beating Blackburn and they stayed there by thrashing Ipswich at Anfield. United therefore finished third after drawing their last match 0–0 with Charlton.

Diego Forlan (centre) takes on Arsenal.

May 2002

The match the nation had been waiting to see – United versus Arsenal – finally came around in the final week of the season. The Gunners already had one trophy in the bag, after beating Chelsea 2–0 in the FA Cup Final. United, meanwhile, were heading for a summer with no silverware to polish … unless they could beat Arsenal at Old Trafford and stretch the title race to one more nerve-jangling day.

The atmosphere inside the Theatre of Dreams was electric as the majority of fans in the 67,850 crowd sang, chanted and roared for the Reds in their quest for victory. In the end, their very vocal efforts were in vain. Cool as you like, Sylvain Wiltord latched on to a loose ball by Mikael Silvestre, raced into the United area and then scored on the rebound after Freddie Ljungberg's shot had been saved by Fabien Barthez. Fifty-five minutes gone, United were 0–1 down. That's the way it stayed until the final whistle and

Mikael Silvestre races past Arsenal midfielder Ray Parlour.

It was a disappointing end to what had been such a dramatic season. But as the United fans clapped their heroes off the Old Trafford pitch for the last time in 2001/02, they heard a message of hope from the manager. Seizing the stadium microphone, Sir Alex Ferguson said to the crowd: "We'll be fighting for you again next season." Glad to hear it, Boss, and rest assured – the readers of this annual will be right behind you!

Premiership (Top six)	P	W	D	L	F	A	Pts
1. Arsenal	38	26	9	3	79	36	87
2. Liverpool	38	24	8	6	67	30	80
3. Manchester United	38	24	5	9	87	45	77
4. Newcastle United	38	21	8	9	74	52	71
5. Leeds United	38	18	12	8	53	37	66
6. Chelsea	38	17	13	8	66	38	64

Can You Win The

The object of this board game is to manage Manchester United to glory in the FA Cup, the Premier League and the European Cup, all in one season … just like Sir Alex Ferguson did in 1999.

Players: You can play the game either on your own or with friends. All you will need to play is some dice (showing numbers one to six) and small items such as coins or buttons that can be used as counters, one per person. If you are playing on your own, you will also need a watch or a clock to time yourself.

Kick-off: Each person must place their counter on square one and determine the order of play by rolling a dice. The person rolling the highest score goes first, the next highest second, and so on. Then, taking it in turns, each person must roll the dice and move their counter across the board by the number of squares shown on the dice. There are three types of square on the board – blank, match and player (see below).

Blank squares: If you land on a blank square after rolling the dice, that's fine. Stay where you are and give the dice to the next player.

Match squares: If you land on a match square, you must answer a question. To determine which question you must answer, turn to page 29 and roll the dice twice. The first roll will decide which set of questions you must select from, the second roll selects the actual question. If you answer the question correctly, then well done – you've won the match and can stay where you are. If you answer the question incorrectly, then you've lost the match and must move back four squares. Note: the person asking the question must keep the correct answer secret if the wrong answer is given. The question might come up again!

Player squares: If you land on a player's named square read the message on that square, then move forwards or backwards the number of squares specified.

Full time: The game finishes when a person answers a question correctly after landing on the European Cup Final match square. The person aiming for the European Cup Final square must roll the exact number of spaces they need on the dice … if the number they roll is too high, they must stay where they are and play passes to the next person.

If you are playing on your own, the game finishes when the time limit of 15 minutes is up. Check the rating for the square you finish on.

SEE PAGE 60 FOR RATINGS.

MANCHESTER UNITED START	**2**	**3**	
11 FOURTH ROUND MATCH	**12**	**13** FIFTH ROUND MATCH	**1**
21 FA CUP FINAL MATCH	**22** DAVID BECKHAM Injures Foot Move back 6	**23**	**2**
31 CHELSEA MATCH	**32**	**33** NICKY BUTT Red Card Move back 10	**3**
41 ARSENAL MATCH	**42** RYAN GIGGS Injures Hamstring Move back 5	**43**	**4**
51 PAUL SCHOLES Red Card Move back 10	**52**	**53** QUARTER FINAL MATCH	**5**

Treble?

1	 5	**RUUD VAN NISTELROOY** 6 New Contract Move forward 5	**THIRD ROUND MATCH** 7	8	**FABIEN BARTHEZ** 9 Saves Penalty Move forward 10	 10
4	**GARY NEVILLE** 15 Scores Own Goal Move back 5 	 16	**QUARTER FINAL MATCH** 17	**JUAN SEBASTIAN VERON** 18 Scores Hat-trick Move forward 5	19	**SEMI FINAL MATCH** 20
4	**MANCHESTER CITY MATCH** 25	 26	**DIEGO FORLAN** 27 Scores Hat-trick Move forward 5	**LEEDS UNITED MATCH** 28	29	30
4	**NEWCASTLE UNITED MATCH** 35	36	**LIVERPOOL MATCH** 37	38	**ROY KEANE** 39 Scores Hat-trick Move forward 5	 40
4	**QUALIFYING ROUND MATCH** 45	46	**GROUP PHASE 1 MATCH** 47	 48	**OLE GUNNAR SOLSKJAER** 49 Scores Hat Trick Move forward 5	**GROUP PHASE 2 MATCH** 50
4	55	**SEMI FINAL MATCH** 56	57	**WES BROWN** 58 Scores Own Goal Move back 5	 59	**EUROPEAN CUP FINAL MATCH** 60

Beckham

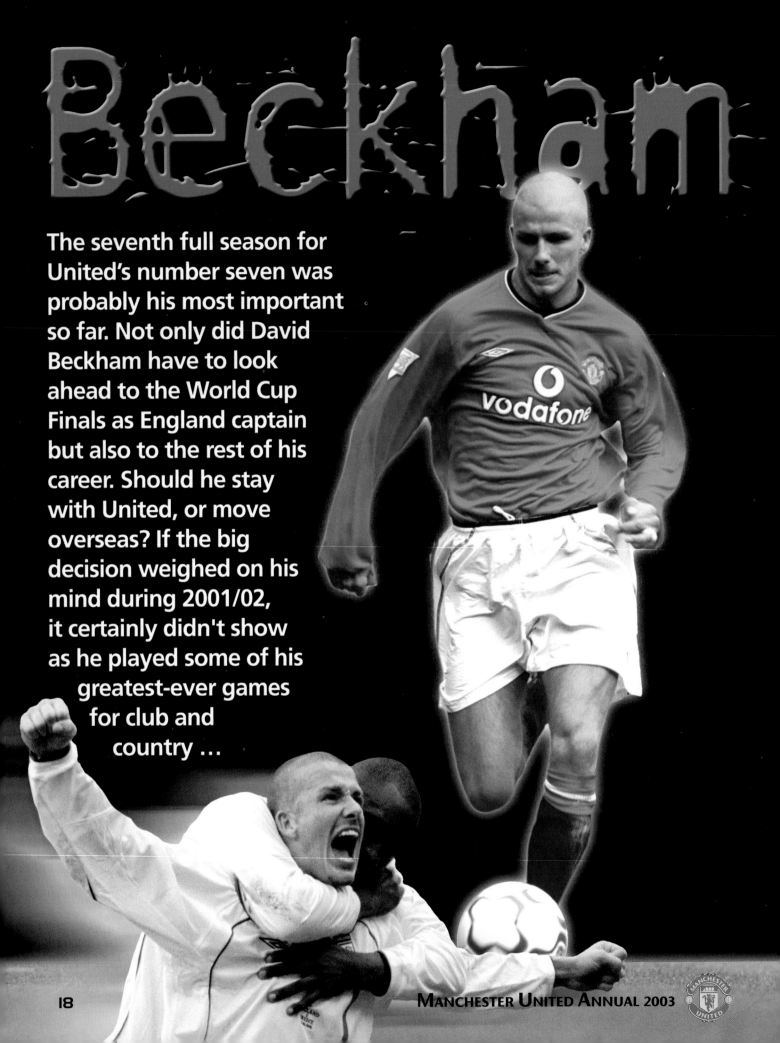

The seventh full season for United's number seven was probably his most important so far. Not only did David Beckham have to look ahead to the World Cup Finals as England captain but also to the rest of his career. Should he stay with United, or move overseas? If the big decision weighed on his mind during 2001/02, it certainly didn't show as he played some of his greatest-ever games for club and country …

B is for Brooklyn

Not only is David a football superhero, he's also a devoted father and husband. Recent TV programmes have shown just how important family life is to the United and England ace, who enjoys nothing more than spending time with his wife Victoria and their first son Brooklyn. They have two homes, in Cheshire – so David can be close to Carrington and Old Trafford – and the other in Hertfordshire. By the time you read this Brooklyn could have a new baby sister or brother to play with in both houses …

E is for England

His second favourite team! Actually, it would be very difficult for David to decide between his club and his country, he takes great pride from playing for both. Being captain of the national side is something he takes very seriously, as millions of people could see when he played out of his skin against Greece at Old Trafford in October 2001. He wanted to make sure England qualified for the 2002 World Cup Finals, and they did so, thanks to the stunning free-kick goal he scored in the dying seconds of an emotional match.

C is for Contract

The tabloid newspapers never get bored of publishing David Beckham's name and photo, whether it's on the front cover, in the fashion section or on the back pages where he truly belongs. The biggest sports story during 2001/02 seemed to be the "will he stay at United?" saga. While David and his advisers quite rightly kept their meetings with United very private, all the papers could do was guess whether he would agree to a new contract with the club or turn it down and leave Old Trafford. Now we know the truth – he's staying!

K is for Kick

As in free-kick, not the sort of kick that landed Becks in trouble during the 1998 World Cup! Scoring goals from set-pieces has always been one of David's special skills, but he seems to be getting better at it from one season to the next. Not only did he net the crucial equaliser for England

against Greece, he also curled in some beauties for United against Fulham, Blackburn, Olympiakos, Southampton, Sunderland and Nantes. A new film about a female footballer even paid tribute to him in its title, *Bend It Like Beckham*.

H is for Hairstyle

If David's contract was the number one priority for the papers in 2001/02, his hairstyle wasn't far behind! One newspaper even used a full page to predict some of the different styles he might wear during the World Cup, from the ponytail made famous by David Seaman, to a new crew cut featuring the cross of St George. Such

BBC Sports Personality of the Year.

wacky stories are like water off a duck's back for David Beckham. It's like he once said himself, to *United* magazine, "At the end of the day, it's what you do on the pitch that counts. Not how you look."

A is for Awards

No wonder David has two homes, he needs all the space to store his awards and medals! Two of the prizes he picked up during 2001/02 were from the viewers of BBC Television. First they named him Sports Personality of the Year, then he received the Best Sporting Moment award for the

England free-kick. David was also proud to be nominated for the World and European Footballer of the Year awards again. This time he was voted second best in the world behind Portugal's Luis Figo, and fourth in Europe (Michael Owen was first).

M is for Manchester

Not Milan or Madrid, where David Beckham is concerned. Any hopes that the top teams in Italy or Spain had of signing the England star were shattered when he told *United* magazine, "My heart is at Old Trafford. I want to go on playing here." In the same interview, David talked about his affection for United fans, who backed him up in 1998 when others were criticising him following his red card in the World Cup. "United fans were the ones, along with my family, who got me through." Let's hope the affection lasts forever!

Fact File

Born: Leytonstone, 2 May 1975
Position: Midfield
Signed for United:
8 July 1991 (trainee)
23 January 1993 (professional)
United Record: 310 (+ 32 sub) games, 74 goals
England Record: 49 games, 6 goals

Statistics correct at the end of the 2001/02 Premiership season.

Becks gives Chelsea's Carlo Cudicini a close shave!

Training-Ground Secrets

Manchester United's training ground is hi-tech, top notch and state of the art. It's also hard to find and difficult to get into unless you have an "access all areas" pass … in other words, permission from Sir Alex! So consider this a privilege, reader, as we take a sneaky look behind the scenes at Carrington.

Welcome to Carrington, the home of present and future stars.

Officially called the Trafford Training Centre, the club's Carrington complex opened for business in January 2000 when the United squad returned from the FIFA Club World Championships in Brazil. The plush premises were instantly popular with the players, coaches, medical and administration staff … it's just as well – the complex cost over £14 million to build!

First-class Facilities

The Trafford Training Centre is one of the best football training grounds in Europe, if not the world.

It boasts a state-of-the-art gymnasium, which cost £80,000 alone and includes an oxygen room where any training or playing conditions can be recreated. There's also a

20

Carrington is equipped with all kinds of fitness aids, including a pool (left) **and a gym** (above).

swimming pool, sauna, steam room and indoor sports hall where injured players can be rehabilitated. Everything a player needs to stay fit! The outdoor facilities are also impressive, with fourteen pitches of varying size spread over 70 acres of land.

Catering for Kids

Opened in July 2002, the Academy Centre at Carrington is used by all the club's junior teams, from the Under-9s to Under-19s, and is situated close to where the first team stars like David Beckham and Roy Keane train.

"Some clubs have their academy centres and first-team training grounds in different locations," explains training ground manager Clive Snell. "But we built our academy centre just across the car park from the main building. That will give the kids a great incentive to make it into the first team here."

The Academy Centre has two synthetic pitches – one indoor, one outdoor – eleven changing rooms, storage space for kits, meeting rooms … in fact it has everything that a coach could possibly want. There's a good reason for that – the centre was modelled on guidelines from the Premier League and ideas from the coaching staff.

The sports hall at Carrington.

The Academy Centre was also designed with parents in mind. While the youngsters play, their relatives can sit and relax in the viewing areas and lounges. And if anyone gets hurt, don't worry – the centre also has its own medical facilities, not to mention highly qualified medical staff.

The Academy Centre cost £8 million to build … so that's a total of £22 million spent on the full Carrington site. Wow!

Training Centre Secrets

United staff travelled the world to get ideas from other football clubs so that Carrington would be the best training ground ever seen. One invention that the club saw at Bayern Munich was a boot-dryer – it's a machine with lots of hooks on the outside. You hang the boots on the hooks, turn it on and it dries the insides of boots after they've been washed. Kitmen Albert Morgan and Alec Wylie wanted one – so they got one!

All the boots are kept in a special cupboard at Carrington, in order of the players' training numbers. Training numbers are different from the players' shirt numbers: that caused some controversy when Juan Sebastian Veron was seen wearing a training top with number seven on it, and people thought it meant that David Beckham had been sold!

Some mischievous soul has glued a pound coin to the path that leads from the players' car park to the dressing room. If you're lucky enough to visit Carrington, don't get caught out by the prank, or you could find all the squad watching and giggling!

Reception at Carrington is a hive of activity on Friday lunch-times – that's when the manager sees the press ahead of the weekend's game. The daily newspapers go first, then the Sundays. Then it's the turn of

the radio reporters, and finally MUTV get to speak to the Boss in their purpose-built studio. It's been known for the manager to sit down with journalists and then tell them all to leave because they've written something he didn't like during the week!

Fabien Barthez had a slight problem the first time he tried to find Carrington after signing from Monaco. The French goalkeeper missed the motorway exit, and ended up in Liverpool. Luckily he found it the next day!

Another new arrival, Juan Sebastian Veron, had a shock when he first arrived at the training ground – David Beckham was sitting on reception! The players often sign cards that have been sent in at the front desk, and Seba breathed a sigh of relief when it was explained that he wouldn't have to welcome guests and answer the phone!

MUTV sometimes interviews players on the upstairs balcony at Carrington. Next time you're watching, listen out in the background for team-mates trying to put off their pals as they're talking on TV!

The official Manchester United magazine uses Carrington as a location for photo shoots with players. One famous shoot involved Ryan Giggs walking across water in the swimming pool – told you he was special!

Facts & Figures

There are **2.4** kilometres of fencing surrounding the training ground – perfect for keeping snooping eyes from Liverpool and Arsenal out.

When the pitches were laid, **100,000** tonnes of sand were brought into Carrington so the grass would be up to United's normal standards.

200,000 tonnes of stones were used to create the paths outside the base.

210,000 litres of diesel fuel were used by vehicles and equipment around the site during construction. Imagine all the free gifts they must have got from the garage for buying all that!

47,000 metres of cables were used to power the **1,300** lights in the complex. We can't have the players training in the dark!

Giggs

Time flies when you're having fun … and ten exciting years seem to have elapsed very quickly since **Ryan Giggs** first played for Manchester United. In 2001/02, he celebrated his testimonial season with the **Reds** but far from being an old-timer, he's still approaching the peak of his powers. Here's our tribute to Ryan, one of the world's greatest wingers …

W is for Wales

Ryan's home nation, as he's very quick to remind people. As a boy born in Cardiff, he used to dream of playing for Wales, and as it turned out, he didn't have long to wait! In October 1991, he became the youngest-ever player to pull on the Welsh jersey when he made his debut against West Germany. He was only 17 years and 321 days old. Less than two years later he scored his first goal for Wales against Belgium. Then in 2001, under the management of his former Manchester United colleague Mark Hughes, Ryan became captain of his country. "Not many players can say they've done that," he told United magazine proudly.

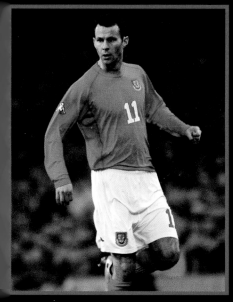

Ryan is proud to wear the red shirt of Wales.

I is for Injuries

Sorry … it would have been nice to pick a more positive word but hamstring injuries have been part and parcel of Ryan's career. Through time, he's learned how to cope with the problem and to do what he can to keep himself on the field and out of the treatment room. He does special exercises, not just before and after every match, but also before and after every training session. This routine requires Ryan to be patient and he's probably the last player to shower and change! It's worth it, though – he knows that if he misses games, the team can miss out on trophies, as they did when he was injured in 1997/98.

N is for November

Probably Ryan's favourite month of the year, apart from May of course when he often collects medals and trophies as a Manchester United player. For a kick-off, he celebrates his birthday on 29 November. In 2003, he'll turn the grand old age of 30 … hope we're invited to the party, it should be a cracker. Other happy anniversaries for Ryan in November include the day when he scored United's fastest-ever goal against Southampton (18 November 1995). Also there is the night when he received a brand new car, after being named Man of the Match in United's Inter-Continental Cup victory in Tokyo (30 November 1999).

G is for Goals

Ryan is best known as a goal-provider, either crossing the ball in from the left wing or feeding a pass through a forest of legs to allow United's strikers to hammer the ball in. But he's also been known to score himself from time to time, often in spectacular fashion! The famous solo run and finish against Arsenal in the 1999 FA Cup semi-final replay is still regarded as one of the greatest goals of all time; he also scored in the Champions League semi-final that season, against Juventus. Playing a few games as a free-to-roam striker in 2001/02 increased Ryan's prospects as a goal-scorer – in fact, he scored nine, to leave him just one short of his United 100.

E is for England

Ryan has spent his entire club career playing in England, and he sees no reason why that should change. Some of the big Italian and Spanish teams would no doubt like to sign him, but Ryan believes he's already playing for the best club in the best league. He loves playing in England, but doesn't regret for one second that he can't play for the national team

… even if Sven Goran Eriksson wishes he could. OK, so Ryan captained England when he was a schoolboy in Salford, but ever since he turned professional, he's been a Welsh international and a very proud one as well! Dream on, Mr Eriksson.

R is for Red

To think he was nearly a Blue! Yes, it's true, Ryan had been on Manchester City's books just before his big break with United came along. Bitter Blues fans will tell you he was stolen from under their noses, but in actual fact, the Maine Road club had released him, so it was their tough luck when Alex Ferguson followed up a lead given to him by a club steward named Harold Wood. The manager called round at Ryan's house and so started the process of turning him into one of the world's best wingers! More than a decade later, Ryan is still a Red and very likely to remain one until the end of his career.

Ryan races past the challenge of Chelsea's Frank Lampard.

Meet the Stars of

MUTV

MUTV, Manchester United's own television channel, was launched in September 1998 to bring Reds fans in more than forty countries closer to the club they love.

The stars of **Reds@Five**, in order of importance: Redford (right), Redford's grandad (left) and Barney (centre).

Several years on, MUTV's biggest star isn't Fabien Barthez, Ryan Giggs, or even David Beckham. No, the biggest star on **MUTV** is Redford, the handsome and intelligent presenter of the popular kids show, **Reds@Five**. With autograph book in hand, we went along to meet him and his human assistant Barney …

A black stretch limousine pulls up outside Old Trafford, and a small crowd gather to see which of United's superstars will emerge. Will it be Becks? Or Ruud? No, it's Redford, lifelong United fan and star of his own TV show.

Just behind the limo pulls up a battered old taxi, from which steps Barney, Redford's co-presenter. While Redford signs autographs and has pictures taken with his adoring public, Barney walks to the dressing room, where their show is filmed, all alone. It's clear who the star is.

A short while later the behind-the-scenes team are going through the show's script with Barney, while Redford enjoys the hour of "Quiet Time" he has written into his contract with United. He cannot be disturbed while he prepares for his performance.

"I've been a United fan all my life," said Redford when we grabbed him for a quick chat. "I'm friends with all the players now, of course, and they all come round my house for tea when they're not playing."

"I'm always very confident, and I always predict that they will win every match 10–0. My grandad, who is on the show sometimes, was here for the match against Anderlecht that United won 10–0, and I think they'll always do that.

"I always go to the matches at Old Trafford, but sometimes I have, erm, appointments, and that means I can't go. I have been to a game, though. I have!"

Along with Damien the bat, Tom the spider and Bob the rabbit, Redford hosts the half-hour show which is crammed with celebrity chat, quickfire quizzes, soccer skills and phone-in competitions – with a little help from Barney, of course.

"Redford is the ultimate professional," Barney told us, reading from a script Redford had given him. "I understand that he needs time on his own before facing the cameras. I much prefer to hang out with the crew and just get on with things, but to be fair to Redford he has taught me so much about presenting, and about life itself too."

The show is chaotic, with prizes and scripts being thrown round the room, and Barney battling to get a word in edgeways as his red friend hogs the airwaves. After half an hour of lunacy, Redford retires to his custom-built jacuzzi, while Barney is led out of the building by security.

Tune into **Reds@Five** on MUTV, every weekday at 5 pm, to catch Redford and Barney's latest adventures.

Presenter Profiles

Barney
Age: 31
Fave Player of All Time: Mark Hughes
Fave United Game Ever: Champions League Final '99
Worst Reds@Five moment: When City fan Carl Bass broke on to set and tried to wrestle Barney to the floor.

Birthplace: Manchester
Fave Player of Present Team: Ryan Giggs/Gary Neville
Best Reds@Five moment: Interviewing Eric Cantona

Redford
Age: Unknown
Fave Player of All Time: Changes every day. On a Monday it's Ryan Giggs, Tuesday is Mark Hughes, Wednesday is David Beckham. He doesn't have one for Thursday and Friday's player is Ruud Van Nistelrooy.

Birthplace: Again unknown but he claims to come from Rochdale, Manchester
Best Reds@Five moment: Making Barney wear a dress on set when it was his birthday.
Worst Reds@Five moment: When Barney got his contract renewed.

Other shows on MUTV

Despite Redford denying it, **MUTV** does show some other programmes. These include:

The Match – All of United's Premiership matches are shown in full on **MUTV**. Saturday matches are first shown at midnight on Sunday, Sunday matches are first shown at 10pm on Monday and games played in midweek are first shown at midnight on the evening they are played!

Red Hot News is filmed from a studio inside Old Trafford, and brings you the most up-to-date news, views and interviews from the club every night at 6 pm.

Inside View is recorded at Carrington the day after every Premiership match, and features one of the key players from the game talking the viewers through the 90 minutes – only on **MUTV** do you get the stars telling you how United won the game.

Reserves Live – if you're a true United fan you know about more than just the first team. The Reserves is the breeding ground for the stars of tomorrow, and **MUTV** shows every league match the kids play. Now you can tell your mates who will be playing for United in five years time!

MUTV is available on cable and satellite TV, such as Sky or NTL. To subscribe in the UK, call **0870 901 0902**. For other countries, see www.mutv.com for details.

Keane

To the majority of fans, he's known as **Keano**. But to the Stretford End faithful at Old Trafford, Roy Keane has always and will always be known simply as **"Massive"**. His nickname is a tribute to the influence he has on games and the immense respect that match-going fans have for the club captain.

M is for Manager

Many fans and pundits see Roy Keane as Sir Alex Ferguson's representative both on and off the pitch. As captain he's the first to speak up when things aren't going right during matches, and no one escapes Roy's wrath if mistakes are made. He's no less outspoken away from the field of play, either, having backed up the manager's criticisms of the team's form and of the sometimes subdued Old Trafford atmosphere. No one would complain if Roy were to take the manager's reigns when Sir Alex decides to hang up his stopwatch. M is also for Maurice, Roy's middle name.

A is for Ailments

When Roy came off worse from a clash with Leeds United's Alf Inge Haaland in 1997/98, it not only ended his season but also United's. The club ended up not winning the Premiership for only the second time since 1993, and Roy's absence was no coincidence. He was also missed in the 2001/02 season – without Roy the team slipped to a home defeat against Middlesbrough that seriously harmed their chances of winning the League again, after having recovered from a terrible start to the season.

S is for Sixteen

Roy has worn the number sixteen shirt ever since joining the Reds from Nottingham Forest in the summer of 1993 for a then British record fee of £3.75 million. Roy's had the chance to pick a squad number between one and eleven but has always declined because of the amount of United replica shirts in Ireland that would instantly become out of date.

S is for Skinhead

Roy says that he shaves his hair off "to keep my head cool in summer", but the psychological effect of the sight of a bald Keane can also be devastating on opponents. His hard-man image has served him well in the past, but it's something he doesn't take too seriously himself - even mocking it in TV adverts by knitting and dressing up as a leprechaun.

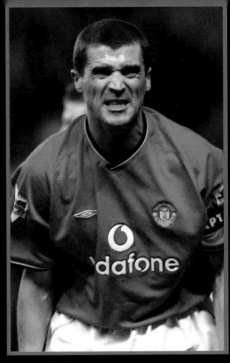

Keano dishes it out!

"I do have a sense of humour, although it might not come across very often. When I'm out on the pitch I'm just concentrating on my job. I think it's important that you do have a laugh and take the mickey out of yourself. Away from football I like to have a laugh and relax just like anyone else," he told ManUtd.com in October 2001.

Roy Keane – Ireland v Holland, September 2001

I is for Ireland

(Republic of). Roy made his debut for his country in 1991, when he was still a young player at Nottingham Forest. Ten years later, he earned his fiftieth cap against Cyprus and celebrated by scoring two goals. That performance was one of several which helped Ireland to qualify for the 2002 World Cup Finals; sadly when the time came to play in the tournament itself, Roy had a row with his national team manager Mick McCarthy and he was kicked out before a ball had been kicked!

V is for Versatile

Roy is much more than a box-to-box midfielder. He has filled in at the centre of defence on numerous occasions, and has expressed the desire to finish his career by playing at sweeper. Roy can also be deadly in attack, as he proved in the Champions League semi-finals of 1999 and 2002. He'd probably make a brilliant goalkeeper too if Fergie asked him to play there!

E is for Europe

Roy seems to save his best performances for the big games, and they don't come much bigger than Champions League clashes. The most impressive show Roy has put on in a red shirt is probably in the away match against Juventus as United marched towards the Treble. Keane was inspirational as the lads won the match 3–2 after having gone 2–0 down early on. Suspension kept him out of the final, though, and he's on a mission to get there with United again.

Fact File

Born: Cork, 10 August 1971
Position: Midfielder
Signed for United: 19 July 1993 (from Nottingham Forest)
United Record: 348 (+ 12 sub) games, 47 goals
Ireland Record: 58 games, 9 goals

Statistics correct at the end of the 2001/02 Premiership season.

MY PERFECT

MU PLAYER

Great football managers like **Sir Alex Ferguson** build their teams from a pool of talented players. Each individual has special abilities, from the agile and acrobatic goalkeeper to the quick and clinical striker.

But just imagine if Sir Alex could ask some top scientists to help him create one perfect player … a player who has the full range of different skills that you normally would find only in a full team! Would that player, **the perfect Manchester United player**, be anything like this?

The Head of Laurent Blanc
Laurent's head would be perfect. Not only does the French defender use his head to clear crosses and high balls into the area, he's also been known to knock in the odd goal from free-kicks and corners. His head also comes with an experienced football brain and a pair of eyes that can read the game brilliantly.

Your choice:

The Shoulders of Roy Keane
When the going gets tough, Roy gets going. He shoulders the responsibility when United are under pressure, making it his duty to carry the team forward and cajole any players who aren't giving their all. When battling for the ball, his shoulders become a barrier to opponents, barging them out of the way, fairly and squarely.

Your choice:

The Hands and Arms of Fabien Barthez
Just in case our perfect player has to go in goal! Fabien's famous fingers, with or without those white gloves, would be ever ready to tip the ball around the post or over the crossbar. His arms, meanwhile, would stretch above an army of opposition players to pluck a dangerous cross from out of the sky.

Your choice:

The Right Foot of David Beckham
No perfect, scientifically created footballer would be complete without the best right boot in English football. It's the foot that can do anything – pass long and short, shoot from inside or outside the box, take corners and free-kicks. Other specialities include bending the ball around a wall and into the top corner.

Your choice:

The Chest of Juan Sebastian Veron
Seba Veron is brilliant at keeping the ball low and under his control. His chest is one of the body parts he uses to cushion a pass from Becks or Keano before launching an attack into the opposition's penalty area. His chest also contains his heart and his lungs, both of which work overtime when he's playing in midfield.

Your choice:

The Hips of Ruud van Nistelrooy
Like the rock and roll legend Elvis Presley, Ruud has rotary hips! At least that's how it seems when the ball's at his feet and his back is facing the goal. Then, all of a sudden, with a spin of those hips, the hitman from Holland can turn to surprise the keeper with a lethal shot. Ruud's hips would help in tight situations.

Your choice:

The Legs of Mikael Silvestre
Mikael Silvestre's legs would give our perfect player a couple of vital attributes. Firstly, speed – enabling the player to race quickly to help a team-mate under pressure or to close down a dangerous striker. Secondly, tackling – Mikael makes perfectly timed slide tackles to steal the ball away from his opponent.

Your choice:

The Left Foot of Ryan Giggs
Please take note, the ball is sold separately! It might look as though it's tied by string to Ryan's left foot, but that's just an illusion, caused by his amazing control. Even when he's running at speed, he keeps the sphere safely in his possession … until it's time to shoot, also with that powerful and famous left foot of his.

Your choice:

Now it's your turn. If you didn't agree with our choice of body parts, simply write a different name in the space provided. But please, don't try this for real! Fergie would prefer to keep his players in one piece.

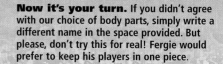

Extra TIME QUIZ

Welcome to this year's quiz page!

There are six sets of six questions, 36 in total, which can be tackled here in their own right or used with the *Can You Win The Treble?* board game on pages 16 and 17. Either way, you'll find the answers on page 60. **Good luck!**

Set 1: Europe
All of the following questions are about the 2001/02 UEFA Champions League.

1. In which country will you find Boavista?
2. Which Spanish team plays its home games at the Riazor?
3. How many goals in total did United score against Deportivo La Coruna?
4. What is the name of the Nantes goalkeeper who frustrated United in France?
5. How many German clubs did United play against?
6. Which Greek club failed to score a single goal against United?

Set 2: The Nineties
Test your memory with these teasers about the last decade.

1. Who scored the winning goal in the 1996 FA Cup final?
2. Which three teams finished above United in 1992, 1995 and 1998?
3. How many Charity Shields did United win during the 1990s?
4. Which club did Brian Kidd join when he left United in 1998?
5. Which three players did Sir Alex Ferguson sign at the start of 1998/99?
6. Name the four Norwegian players who played for United in the 1990s.

Set 3: Old Trafford
The answers to the following questions are all compass points.

1. At which end of the ground will you find the Sir Matt Busby statue?
2. Which stand is on the site of the old Stretford End terrace?
3. On which side of the pitch will you find the manager's bench and the press box?
4. Which of the four stands has the largest number of seats in it?
5. Which two stands meet in the away fans corner?
6. On which side of the ground will you find the Museum and the Red Café?

Set 4: Premiership
All of the following questions are based on the 2001/02 Premiership season.

1. Where did Roy Carroll make his debut for Manchester United?
2. What record did Ruud van Nistelrooy set when he scored a penalty against Blackburn?
3. Why couldn't Ole Gunnar Solskjaer take the match-ball home after his hat-trick at Bolton?
4. What was the final score when United played at Charlton, and who scored the goals?
5. Who played his last game for United when they lost 1–0 at home to West Ham?
6. What was special about Juan Sebastian Veron's goal against Everton at Old Trafford?

Set 5: Internationals
These questions are all about the international careers of your favourite players.

1. Which country did Ryan Giggs captain when he was a schoolboy?
2. Name the United star who plays his international home games at Windsor Park.
3. Who earned his first cap for Scotland in April 2002?
4. Which two United players faced each other at the Millennium Stadium in 2001/02?
5. Which two countries did David Beckham score against at Old Trafford during 2001/02?
6. Which United star played for his country at the 2000 Olympics in Sydney?

Set 6: The Manager
How much do you know about Sir Alex Ferguson?

1. Which club in Glasgow did Sir Alex play for?
2. What is the name of his wife?
3. Which of his three sons used to play for United?
4. Which other sport is Sir Alex actively involved in?
5. In which month and year did he become the United manager?
6. What was the first trophy Sir Alex won with the Reds?

Six
of the
Best

Ruud van Niste... ...van Nistelrooy
Ruud van Nistelrooy ...Ruud van Nistelrooy
Ruud van Nistelroo... ...lrooy
Ruud van Nistelroo... ...van Nistelrooy
Ruud van N... ...roo... ...Nistelrooy

Ruud van Nistelrooy had a fantastic first season with Manchester United. Not only did he break the Premiership record by scoring in eight matches in a row, he also broke the hearts of a few goalkeepers too! Here's our tribute to the Dutch master's work during 2001/02, six of the best league games that featured his goals ...

1 – 0 Middlesbrough
Riverside Stadium
15 December 2001
Goal! van Nistelrooy 75

One of the most important goals in Ruud's fab first season was the one he scored at Middlesbrough. The Reds were in danger of dropping two more Premiership points until the Dutchman did the business, with only fifteen minutes to spare. Ryan Giggs took a shot, the goalkeeper spilled it, and there was Ruud to snap up the loose ball and blast United back to winning ways away from home. In fact it was the first time Ruud had won a league match on his travels since Tottenham ... and that was a very different game indeed!

2 – 1 Blackburn Rovers
Old Trafford, 19 January 2002
Goals! van Nistelrooy 45 (penalty)
Keane 82

Ruud proved he could take penalties in this game against some familiar faces. Blackburn's team included Andy Cole, who'd only just left the Reds, and the man who used to wear United's number ten shirt, Mark Hughes. The big moment for the new number ten came just before the break, when the score was still 0–0. The home fans held their breath as Ruud put the ball on the spot, then roared as it flew into the net! This goal broke the Premiership record – it was the eighth league game in a row in which Ruud had scored.

3 – 2 Fulham
Old Trafford, 19 August 2001
Goals! Beckham 35
van Nistelrooy 51, 53

For most United fans, this was the first time they'd seen Ruud in a red shirt. And boy, were they impressed! After scoring and playing in a few pre-season friendlies, the first match of the Premiership season was the real deal for the Dutchman. Unfortunately for Fulham, Ruud rose to the occasion superbly, scoring two goals in three minutes to thrill the 67,534 fans inside Old Trafford and the millions at home watching on TV. It was a dream league debut, for Ruud to turn the scoreline round from 2–1 down to 3–2 up.
Super start!

4 – 0 Tottenham Hotspur
Old Trafford, 6 March 2002
Goals! Beckham 15, 64
van Nistelrooy 43 (penalty), 76

The Dutchman grabbed another double in this impressive result against Teddy Sheringham's new team at Old Trafford. The former United striker, now captaining Spurs, could only stand and admire the man who had replaced him in the hearts of the home supporters. Ruud struck first from the penalty spot in the 43rd minute, after Tottenham's Taricco had been sent off for a foul on Paul Scholes. Van The Man later made it 4–0 to United with his second goal of the night, scored in the 76th minute. Tough luck, Teddy!

5 – 0 Derby County
Old Trafford, 12 December 2001
Goals! Solskjaer 6, 58
Keane 10
van Nistelrooy 63
Scholes 89

United's cracking Christmas kicked off with this demolition of Derby County, in which Ruud started alongside Ole Gunnar Solskjaer for only the second time. The deadly duo grabbed three goals between them, to convince Sir Alex they should stick together. Ruud's goal, in the 63rd minute, made the score 4–0, and that's the way it stayed until Scholes squeezed in number five, just a minute from full time. It was a five-star performance and the biggest victory of the season ... well, until the next home game that is!

6 – 1 Southampton
Old Trafford, 22 December 2001
Goals! van Nistelrooy 1, 34, 54
Solskjaer 41
Keane 72
Phil Neville 78

Ruud scored his first hat-trick for the Reds in this wonderful win. It took him less than an hour, starting with a strike inside the very first minute, which he scored from a cross by Scholes. Ruud rattled in his second goal, also in the first half, from a scramble in the Saints area. Then, for his third, he ran clear of the defence and stroked the ball into the net with the outside of his foot, just nine minutes into the second half. It was an awesome performance by the striker ... and still there's the promise of much, much more to come!

DID YOU KNOW?

Ten must be Southampton's unlucky number. For two years in a row, the man wearing the ten shirt for Manchester United – Teddy Sheringham in 2000, then Ruud in 2001 – scored a hat-trick against them at Old Trafford!

Follow Follow Follow

... because United are going to Glasgow!"

At least that's what the Reds fans hoped when Hampden Park in Sir Alex Ferguson's home city was picked to host the 2002 UEFA Champions League Final. The United faithful's "Follow" anthem, based on an old tune called "The Entertainer", echoed around Old Trafford throughout the season. But how did the most entertaining side in England fare in Europe?

Phase One, Group G

United had to negotiate a first phase full of surprises. Like Lille, the little-fancied French side who were heading for a shock draw at Old Trafford until David Beckham broke their hearts. His last-minute goal made it 1–0 to United. The next surprise package was opened up in Spain where Deportivo la Coruna, after trailing to a superb first-half strike by Paul Scholes, suddenly turned the game on its head in the last four minutes. Naybet and Pandiani provided the sting in the tail, Deportivo won 2–1.

United were shell-shocked but they bounced back on their next overseas adventure. Wearing gold, the Reds beat Olympiakos 2–0 in Athens thanks to Becks again and Andy Cole, the club's all-time top scorer in the competition. He finished his career at United with 19 European Cup goals ... it's just a shame he had to finish it in mid-season!

Juan Sebastian Veron takes on Sylvain N'Diaye of Lille in the 2001/02 UEFA Champions League.

The man who could eventually break Andy Cole's record, Ruud van Nistelrooy, scored twice against Deportivo in Manchester. The Spaniards had the last laugh though, mainly at Fabien Barthez who made two blunders in United's 3–2 defeat. The poor result left the Reds needing to win one of their last two games. Thankfully they beat Olympiakos again, 3–0 at home, with late goals by Ole Gunnar Solskjaer, Ryan Giggs and Ruud, who'd earlier missed a penalty. Another surprise!

Ole scored again in United's final Group G game, the 1–1 draw that saw Lille finish third and qualify for the UEFA Cup. The Reds finished second, and would have bigger fish to fry in the next phase …

Phase Two, Group A

The big fish don't come much bigger than Bayern Munich, the club that lost the European Cup to United in 1999, but then won it in 2001 after crushing the Reds in the quarter-finals.

This time, neither heavyweight could knock out the other. Ruud van Nistelrooy and Paulo Sergio scored in the 1–1 stalemate in Munich, sadly no one did in the 0–0 bore draw in Manchester. Both teams went through, after finishing above Boavista and Nantes, the dark horses from Portugal and France.

Boavista and Nantes weren't just there for the ride, however. After battling through Phase One against the odds, they were hoping to upset the favourites again. Nantes came the nearest, leading against United in France from the 9th minute until the 90th when Ruud van Nistelrooy kept his cool to finally level the match, 1–1, from the spot. Scoring from open play had proved impossible against the amazing Nantes goalkeeper, Mickael Landreau!

The outcome at Old Trafford was completely different. This time Landreau's luck totally deserted him, as Beckham, Solskjaer (2), Mikael Silvestre and van Nistelrooy (with another penalty) all scored to give United their biggest win of the campaign, 5–1. All this after Da Rocha had given Nantes da lead! Wicked!

Not only did United put six in total past Nantes, they did the same to Boavista. The Reds won 3–0 at home with goals by Van Nistelrooy (2) and Laurent Blanc, and then 3–0 away thanks to Blanc again, Beckham

Phase One, Group G Table	P	W	D	L	F	A	Pts
1. Deportivo La Coruna	6	2	4	0	10	8	10
2. Manchester United	6	3	1	2	10	6	10
3. Lille	6	1	3	2	7	7	6
4. Olympiakos Piraeus	6	1	2	3	6	12	5

Phase Two, Group A Table	P	W	D	L	F	A	Pts
1. Manchester United	6	3	3	0	13	3	12
2. Bayern Munich	6	3	3	0	5	2	12
3. Boavista	6	1	2	3	2	8	5
4. Nantes	6	0	2	4	4	11	2

(penalty) and Solskjaer. That last result confirmed United as Group A winners and guaranteed them one of the "easier" draws in the quarter-finals – Deportivo la Coruna, Panathinaikos or Liverpool!

Quarter-Finals

From the easier draws on offer, United were handed the most difficult one! Or so it seemed – after all, they had already lost both home and away to their last eight opponents, Deportivo la Coruna. The Reds needed to reverse those first round results – or else be knocked out of the last eight for the third year in a row.

This time, United won, with great determination and with David Beckham dominating the headlines! First, the good news: David's fantastic goal from thirty yards that set United up for their first-ever away win against a Spanish side (Van Nistelrooy's goal made the first leg final score 2–0). Then the bad news: Becks was stretchered off in both the first and second leg matches after terrible tackles by Tristan and Duscher. The second injury was more serious, a broken metatarsal bone in his foot that marked the end of his season.

The man who came on for Beckham in the second leg, super-sub Ole Gunnar Solskjaer, scored two and Giggs grabbed the other to sink Deportivo 3–2 at Old Trafford, 5–2 on aggregate. This meant that Sir Alex Ferguson was now just one step away from that dream final at Hampden Park.

Semi-Finals

United's opponents in the penultimate round were the team that had knocked Liverpool out,

Bayer Leverkusen. The Germans were the underdogs, even though two of United's midfield terriers were missing from the first leg eleven – Becks and Roy Keane, who had also been injured in Spain against Deportivo.

Keano eventually came on as substitute in the first match, but by then United were in trouble. They had twice taken the lead, through Zivkovic's own goal and Van Nistelrooy's penalty, only to let Leverkusen back into the tie. It finished 2–2 at Old Trafford, but Bayer had claimed the advantage of two away goals.

Those goals, scored by Ballack and Neuville, proved to be crucial. Keano scored first for United in Germany, tucking the ball in from a tight angle after going round the goalkeeper. But then Neuville rocketed his second goal of the semi-final to make it 1–1 on the night, 3–3 on aggregate.

Bayer Leverkusen went through to their first-ever final on the away goals rule, but only after some desperate defending that included four goal-line clearances. The last of these was a header to deny Diego Forlan's shot – had that gone in, United would have gone to Glasgow. It just wasn't to be … but maybe next year will be different. The 2003 final is at Old Trafford, after all.

Ryan races towards goal against Olympiakos.

South American Idols

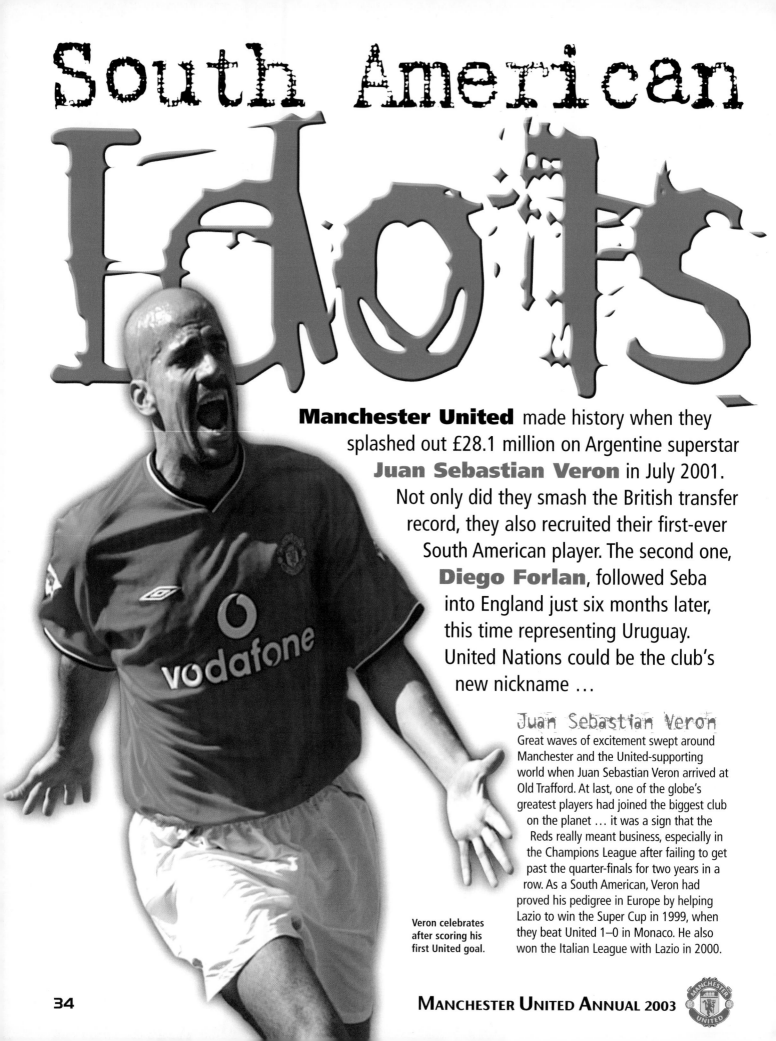

Manchester United made history when they splashed out £28.1 million on Argentine superstar **Juan Sebastian Veron** in July 2001. Not only did they smash the British transfer record, they also recruited their first-ever South American player. The second one, **Diego Forlan**, followed Seba into England just six months later, this time representing Uruguay. United Nations could be the club's new nickname …

Juan Sebastian Veron

Great waves of excitement swept around Manchester and the United-supporting world when Juan Sebastian Veron arrived at Old Trafford. At last, one of the globe's greatest players had joined the biggest club on the planet … it was a sign that the Reds really meant business, especially in the Champions League after failing to get past the quarter-finals for two years in a row. As a South American, Veron had proved his pedigree in Europe by helping Lazio to win the Super Cup in 1999, when they beat United 1–0 in Monaco. He also won the Italian League with Lazio in 2000.

Veron celebrates after scoring his first United goal.

MANCHESTER UNITED ANNUAL 2003

Lazio, then managed by Sven Goran Eriksson, were as keen to keep Veron as United were to sign him, hence the high price of £28.1 million. But the record transfer fee didn't concern Seba, he just wanted to get on to the Old Trafford turf and strut his stuff … just like his father, Juan Senior, had done for Estudiantes against United in the 1968 Inter-Continental Cup. His dad defeated legends like Bobby Charlton, George Best and Denis Law … now it was up to Juan Junior to join those great names in Manchester United's hall of fame.

Seba made a great start in his attempt to achieve this. In only his second month in a red shirt, he scored three goals in three terrific games of football against Everton (4–1), Newcastle (3–4) and Tottenham (3–5). His first goal against Everton saw him trading passes with his new midfield partner Roy Keane and then polishing off the move with a majestic shot. But it was Seba's all-round performance which really caught the eye in that game. Sometimes he pinged pinpoint passes across the pitch, at other times he kept the ball to himself to show off his tricks to the Old Trafford crowd. The home fans were awestruck.

The fans who travelled to Tottenham in September saw Seba put on another superb show, but of a slightly different kind. It wasn't so much a pleasure cruise this time, in fact there was no time for showboating as United battled back from 3–0 down to win 5–3. Veron was masterful in the second half, scoring the fourth goal that finally edged the Reds in front.

Veron's great performances didn't start and then stop in September, far from it, but by the end of the season, questions were being asked as to why United hadn't won anything. The easiest answer was to blame Seba, the club's most expensive player. But the critics should take heed from history … the scapegoat for United's last empty season, Teddy Sheringham in 1998, bounced back with a vengeance in 1999. We could well see the same from Seba.

It's a stat: Seba's £28.1m fee was more than the total spent on Jaap Stam, Dwight Yorke and Jesper Blomqvist in 1998!

Diego Forlan

Diego Forlan didn't arrive with quite the same reputation as Juan Sebastian Veron, and the fanfare around the world wasn't so loud … even if the United fans were again quite excited by the arrival of a new striker. Foreign players really seem to inspire supporters. Maybe it's the mysterious element of not knowing what to expect – Ole Gunnar Solskjaer took everyone by surprise, especially opposing defenders, during his first season in England. Or perhaps it's the pedigree of previous imports – Peter Schmeichel and Eric Cantona are regarded as two of English football's greatest-ever players. Whatever the expectations, it's up to the player himself to make sure he lives up to them.

Since the moment he signed in January 2002, Diego Forlan has been fully committed to the cause, playing with the sort of gusto and guile that United fans love to see. The home fans chanted his name when, against Spurs in March, he demonstrated his great control, his accurate passing and his abundance of energy. These qualities came to the fore when he created David Beckham's second goal in the 4–1 win.

In fact, Forlan did everything but score himself. Scoring was something that Diego was desperate to do in his first half-season. The closest he came was in the biggest game of the lot, away to Bayer Leverkusen. With time running out for the Reds in the Champions League semi-final, the ball fell to Forlan just outside the area. Steadying himself, the striker hit a first-time shot that seemed to have "We're in the final" written all over it. The Bayer keeper was in no position to save it, but unfortunately for Forlan and the millions of United fans watching on TV, a defender was in just the right place to head it clear from under the crossbar. It was the first real moment of drama for Diego at United … and unlikely to be his last.

It's a stat: Uruguay was the 13th nation outside of the UK and Ireland to provide a first team player for United. Just for fun, can you name the previous twelve United Nations? The answer is on page 60.

Top: **Fergie welcomes Forlan to Old Trafford.**
Above: **Diego bravely dives in to head the ball.**

Comeback KINGS

Manchester United have a great knack for coming back from the brink of defeat. Here are the key incidents from six classic comebacks, three from 2001/02 and three from the Treble-winning season of 1998/99.

Bayern Munich @ Nou Camp
26 May 1999
UEFA Champions League Final

6': Mario Basler scores for Bayern Munich from a direct free-kick. United are 1–0 down!

Half-time score: Manchester United 0 Bayern Munich 1. The Reds are barely in the match.

67': United substitution #1, Teddy Sheringham on for Jesper Blomqvist.

70': Bayern substitution #1, Mehmet Scholl on for Alexander Zickler.

79': Scholl's shot hits the post. Lucky escape for United.

81': United substitution #2, Ole Gunnar Solskjaer on for Andy Cole.

84': Jancker's shot hits the crossbar. Another close shave for the Reds.

90': Sheringham equalises for United from a shot by Ryan Giggs. 1–1, United are level!

90': Solskjaer scores for United from Sheringham's header. United are 2–1 up!

Full-time score: Manchester United 2 Bayern Munich 1. The Reds have won the Treble!

Juventus @ Stadio delle Alpi
21 April 1999
UEFA Champions League
Semi-final 2nd leg

6': Filippo Inzaghi scores for Juventus. United are 1–0 down!

10': Filippo Inzaghi scores again for Juventus. United are 2–0 down!

24': Roy Keane – by now suspended for the final due to a yellow card – pulls one back for United with a glancing header. United are 2–1 down!

34': Dwight Yorke equalises for United from Cole's cross. 2–2, United are level!

Half-time score: Juventus 2 Manchester United 2. The Reds are now leading the two-legged tie on away goals.

84': Andy Cole scores for United as Yorke's run is halted. United are 3–2 up!

Full-time score: Juventus 2 Manchester United 3. The Reds have reached the final!

Liverpool @ Old Trafford
24 January 1999
FA Cup Fourth Round

3': Michael Owen scores for Liverpool. United are 1–0 down!

Half-time score: Manchester United 0 Liverpool 1. The Reds are heading out of the FA Cup.

81': United substitution #3, Ole Gunnar Solskjaer on for Gary Neville.

88': Dwight Yorke prods the ball over the line to equalise. 1–1, United are level!

90': Ole Gunnar Solskjaer fires in the second goal. United are 2–1 up!

Full-time score: Manchester United 2 Liverpool 1. The Reds have knocked their rivals out of the Cup!

Spurs @ White Hart Lane
29 September 2001
FA Premier League

15': Dean Richards scores for Spurs. United are 1–0 down!

25': Les Ferdinand scores for Spurs. United are 2–0 down!

45': Christian Ziege scores for Spurs. United are 3–0 down!

Half-time score: Tottenham Hotspur 3 Manchester United 0. The Reds are in tatters.

46': Andy Cole scores with a diving header. United are now 3–1 down!

58': Laurent Blanc scores with a towering header. United are now 3–2 down!

72': Ruud van Nistelrooy equalises. 3–3, United are now level!

76': Juan Sebastian Veron scores. Incredible, United are now 4–3 up!

87': David Beckham nets for the Reds. Remarkable, United are now 5–3 up!

Full-time score: Tottenham Hotspur 3 Manchester United 5. The greatest comeback ever!

Aston Villa @ Villa Park
6 January 2002
FA Cup Third Round

Half-time score: Aston Villa 0 Manchester United 0. The Reds are not playing well.

51': Ian Taylor scores for Villa. United are 1–0 down!

53': Phil Neville scores an own goal. United are 2–0 down!

56': United substitution #2, Ruud van Nistelrooy on for Luke Chadwick.

77': Ole Gunnar Solskjaer pulls a goal back. United are now 2–1 down!

80': Van Nistelrooy equalises for the Reds. 2–2, United are now level!

82': Van Nistelrooy scores again. United are now 3–2 up!

Full-time score: Aston Villa 2 Manchester United 3. The Reds go through after bouncing back!

West Ham United @ Upton Park
16 March 2002
FA Premier League

8': Steve Lomas scores for West Ham. United are 1–0 down!

17': David Beckham equalises with a superb shot. 1–1, United are level!

20': Freddie Kanoute scores for West Ham. United are 2–1 down!

22': Nicky Butt equalises with an overhead kick. 2–2, United are level!

Half-time score: West Ham United 2 Manchester United 2. The Reds have twice come from behind.

55': Paul Scholes scores from Ole Gunnar Solskjaer's cross. United are now 3–2 up!

64': Solskjaer scores for the visitors. United are now 4–2 up!

74': West Ham substitution #1, Jermain Defoe on for Nigel Winterburn.

78': Defoe pulls one back for West Ham. United are now 4–3 up!

89': Beckham scores a penalty. United are now 5–3 up!

Full-time score: West Ham United 3 Manchester United 5. The Reds triumph in a see-saw match.

Who Am I?

Who Am I?

Enniskillen is my birthplace.

I moved to England when I was seventeen.

Sammy McIlroy is my international coach.

I made my Premier League debut at Villa Park.

My squad number is unlucky for some.

My name is …

Who Am I?

Bury is my birthplace.

I am exactly two years younger than Nicky Butt.

Cricket is my favourite other sport.

I scored the sixth goal against Southampton last season.

My father's first name is Neville.

My name is …

Who Am I?

Oss is my birthplace.

I officially became a United player on my 25th birthday.

I started my career with Den Bosch.

The other kit I'm proud to wear is orange.

I scored a hat-trick against Southampton last season.

My name is …

The editor of the annual can be a lazy so-and-so sometimes. Here's a feature that he didn't quite finish, so can you help us out and match the profiles on the yellow panels to the photos below?

Who Am I?

Manchester is my birthplace.

I made my first team debut against Leeds United.

My age will match my squad number in October 2003.

I didn't score for United last season.

My first game for England was against Hungary.

My name is …

Who Am I?

Kristiansund is my birthplace.

I used to support Liverpool when I was a kid. (Not any more!)

My first club was called Clausenengen.

I scored a hat-trick against Bolton last season.

My first child's name is Noah.

My name is …

Who Am I?

Cape Town is my birthplace.

I was born on the day United won the FA Cup in 1977.

My previous club was Atletico Madrid.

I scored against Everton last season.

My country played in the 2002 World Cup Finals.

My name is …

The answers are on page 60.

Sir Alex: "Och, I cannae find Denis anywhere. Surely he hasn't left already?"

Giggs: "Don't worry, Denis, we'll keep the gaffer away from you."
Scholes: "Look out lads, he's coming this way!"

Sir Alex: "Is that him, hiding in the press box? Och, no, it's that pesky journalist. Oi, get oot!"

Sir Alex Ferguson wants to give **Denis Irwin** a special leaving present, the Manchester United Annual 2003, but try as he might, he can't find the defender anywhere. Denis, meanwhile, is ducking and diving ... he thinks the manager's present will be boring, like a book about stamp-collecting!

Keane: "Hey, Den, he hasn't got a clue where you are!" (Laughs.)
Veron: "I think we have driven him around ze bend!"
Scholes: "He's lost the plot – just listen to him whistling!"

Sir Alex: "Och, this is getting ridiculous. All I want to do is give Denis his present. I'll try this way."

Keane: "That's it, men, all pile on!"
Denis: "Umph! Steady on, you'll crush me!"

nos?

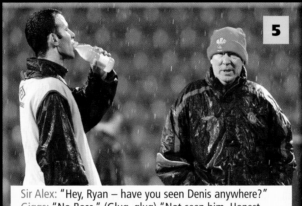

4

Silvestre: "We need to be careful, I think Monsieur Fergie is getting angry."
Butt: "You're spot on. Giggsy, go and stall him."
Giggs: "Righto!"

5

Sir Alex: "Hey, Ryan – have you seen Denis anywhere?"
Giggs: "No Boss." (Glug, glug) "Not seen him. Honest. Have you tried whistling?"

6

Sir Alex: "Great idea, I'll give it a go. Yoo-hoo! Denis!" (Whistles)

9

Denis: "Hang on … maybe he's seen me. He's coming towards us!"
Keane: "Oh no! you're right. Quick, let's hide you!"

10

O'Shea: "He won't see past me, Denis, I'm the tallest man in the squad."
Butt: "I dunno lads, I think we need some more bodies."

12

Sir Alex: "Och, I can only see Keano and the boys messin' aboot. I give up! My horses can have the annual instead, that'll teach Mr Irwin not tae hide from me!"

13

Solskjaer: "He's gone, Denis. The coast is clear."
Keane: "Yep, time to come out, and time you were on your way."
Denis: "Thanks, guys, for everything. It's been nice to know you!"
(From the editor: Thanks for 12 years of loyal service, Denis. Goodbye and good luck.)

FA PREMIE

DATE	OPPOSITION	VENUE	FINAL SCORE

UNITED SCORERS	POINTS	TOTAL	POSITION

YOUR FILL-IN CHART FOR THE 02/03 SEASON

PREMIERSHIP WINNERS

1993
1994
1996
1997
1999
2000
2001

MANCHESTER UNITED ANNUAL 2003

Tracking the 2002/03 campaign

DATE	OPPOSITION	VENUE

LEAGUE CUP MATCHES

	THE MILLENNIUM STADIUM, CARDIFF	

FA CUP MATCHES

	THE MILLENNIUM STADIUM, CARDIFF	

DATE	VENUE	OPPOSITION

UEFA CHAMPIONS LEAGUE MATCHES

	FIRST PHASE	
	SECOND PHASE	
	OLD TRAFFORD, MANCHESTER	

CUP ⚽ CHAMPIONS LEAGUE

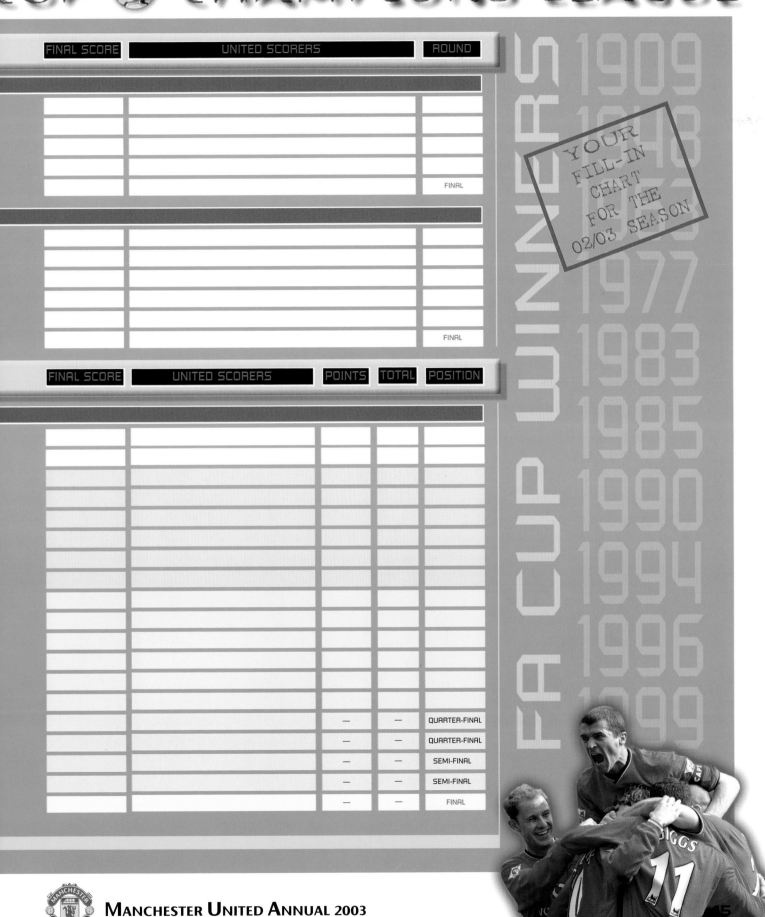

FINAL SCORE	UNITED SCORERS	ROUND
		FINAL
		FINAL

FINAL SCORE	UNITED SCORERS	POINTS	TOTAL	POSITION
		—	—	QUARTER-FINAL
		—	—	QUARTER-FINAL
		—	—	SEMI-FINAL
		—	—	SEMI-FINAL
		—	—	FINAL

FA CUP WINNERS

1909
1977
1983
1985
1990
1994
1996

Golden Future

The live TV cameras caught a glimpse of **Manchester United's** future on 5 November 2001, when **Sir Alex Ferguson** picked eight young men aged 22 or under to play in the Worthington Cup. In this special feature, we profile the golden hopefuls who dared to take on the mighty Arsenal …

John O'Shea

Born: Waterford, Ireland, 30 April 1981
Position: Centre-back

John played the full 90 minutes and was the pick of United's defenders against Arsenal. The 0-4 scoreline might suggest the back four had a nightmare but they were playing against a very experienced strike force in Wiltord and Kanu. There was certainly no shame in O'Shea's performance, and he started again in the first team a few weeks later, alongside Laurent Blanc. Together, the veteran Frenchman and the young Irishman helped United to keep clean sheets in consecutive games against Middlesbrough and Derby County. That's a proud stat for O'Shea; clean sheets were a real rarity for the Reds in 2001/02!

Lee Roche

Born: Bolton, England, 28 October 1980
Position: Right-back

Lee returned to United in 2001/02, having spent all of the previous season on loan to Wrexham. He did very well for the Robins, earning their Young Player of The Year award, but there was never any question of Lee joining them permanently. The quiet but courageous lad still hopes to make it with United, after making his debut at Arsenal. Roche did well enough to stay on the field for the full match, despite being involved in the second goal when Kanu was brought down and Wiltord scored from the spot.

Michael Stewart

Born: Edinburgh, Scotland, 26 February 1981
Position: Centre midfield

Michael made his debut for United in the Worthington Cup, on Halloween Night 2000. He showed no fear in that game at Watford, nor at Arsenal on Bonfire Night 2001. Fireworks are sometimes a part of Stewart's game but he put in a disciplined performance against the Gunners, anchoring the midfield alongside the more attacking Dwight Yorke. Michael would like nothing more than to partner his hero Roy

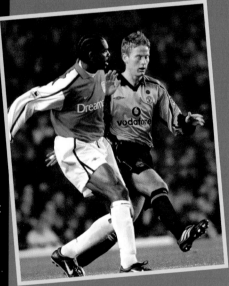

Keane one day. To do that, he'll need to keep following the same path as Nicky Butt and Paul Scholes – they made the grade from youth team to first team in 1995/96.

Luke Chadwick

Born: Cambridge, England, 18 November 1980
Position: Right midfield

Like a lot of young footballers, Luke had a difficult "second season" with United. When 2001/02 kicked off, he was hoping to build on the achievements of the previous year when he played 22 games and scored two goals. In fact, the game against his former club, Arsenal, proved to be one of

the rare nights in the limelight for the England Under-21 winger. The arrival of Juan Sebastian Veron was partly to blame for Luke's lack of appearances – it meant that he was no longer first choice to play whenever David Beckham needed a rest.

Bojan Djordjic

Born: Belgrade, Yugoslavia,
6 February 1982
Position: Left midfield

Bojan was another young winger who had high hopes for a major breakthrough in 2001/02. This followed the end-of-season friendly in May 2001 when he scored a superb goal for the first team against Celtic. Determined not to be a one-goal wonder, Djordjic drove a Beckham-style free-kick over the Arsenal wall in the Worthington Cup match, only to see it cannon off the crossbar! He did the same trick on his debut for Sheffield Wednesday, where he spent some time on loan during 2001/02. All of this suggests there's more to come from the lad from Yugoslavia who plays international football for Sweden.

Danny Webber

Born: Manchester, England,
28 December 1981
Position: Forward

Danny made his debut at Arsenal and almost equalised in the first half when he

sprinted past the home defence for a showdown with Richard Wright. Unfortunately the young England goalkeeper made a good save to deny Danny his moment of glory. Some of the talent scouts must have been impressed by what they saw in Webber. The following month he took time out from scoring goals

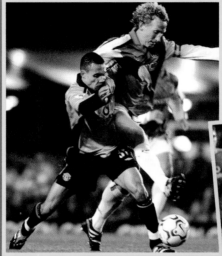

for United Reserves to play first team football on loan at Port Vale. Danny left United again in March to see out the season on loan to Watford. He also played for England during 2001/02, joining Jimmy Davis in the Under-20 team.

Jimmy Davis

Born: Bromsgrove, England,
6 February 1982
Position: Forward

Jimmy isn't just one of United's bright prospects for the future. England are also hoping he can make it in the big time after some fine performances for the national

team at youth level. In March 2002, for example, he scored twice for the Under-20s in their 3–0 win over Finland at Bolton's Reebok Stadium. He wears the number seven shirt for England, and like his hero David Beckham, he's capable of testing goalkeepers with direct free-kicks. Jimmy will be hoping to test himself again in the first team very soon, after making a bright debut against Arsenal.

Daniel Nardiello

Born: Coventry, England, 22 October 1982
Position: Forward

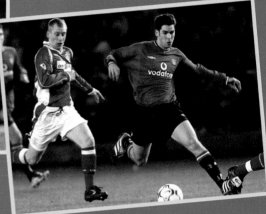

Daniel didn't start the match against Arsenal, so he could only look on and learn as Sylvain Wiltord scored a first-half hat-trick for the home side. Scoring goals is something that Daniel has done often enough at youth level. In 1999/2000, he was top marksman for United's Under-19s with 14 goals. More recently he's been banging them in for the reserves, so a first team debut in the Worthington Cup was no more than he deserved. His big moment came in the 71st minute when he replaced Davis as Webber's strike partner.

The Manager's Verdict

"The pleasing thing for me about the Arsenal game was that we never lost our will to play. We kept playing some nice football, we kept passing the ball and the touch was good from all our players. That's the distinct way in which we expect young Manchester United players to express themselves. I was pleased with that."

SIR ALEX FERGUSON

Pride of LIONS

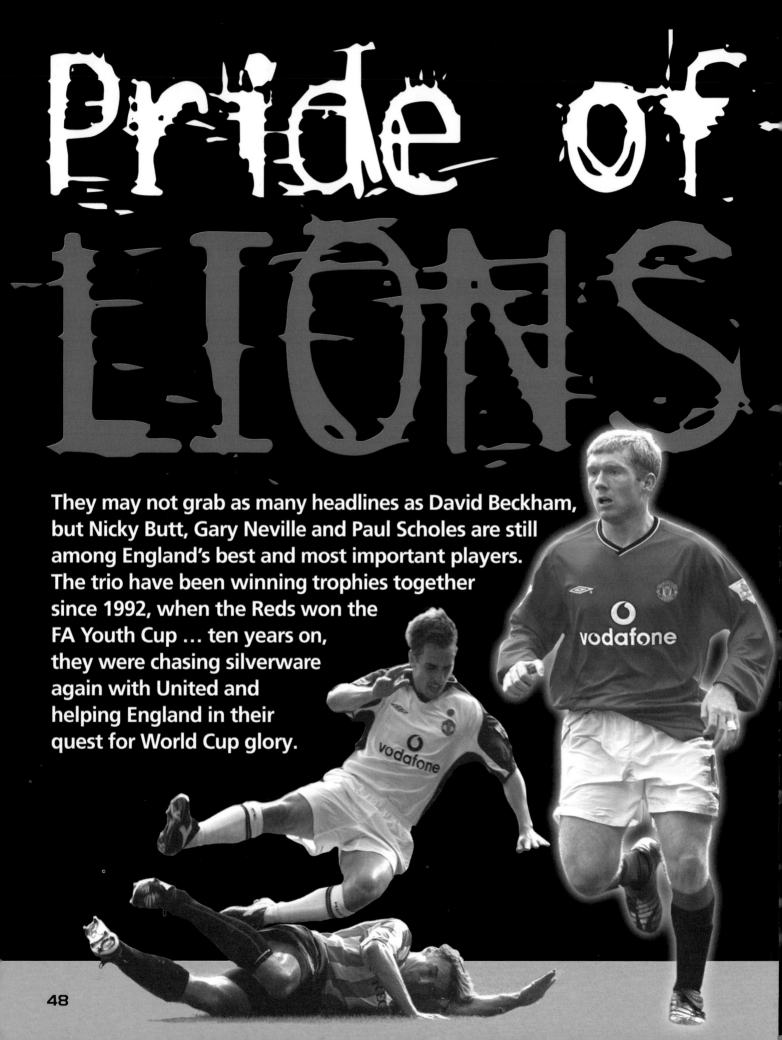

They may not grab as many headlines as David Beckham, but Nicky Butt, Gary Neville and Paul Scholes are still among England's best and most important players. The trio have been winning trophies together since 1992, when the Reds won the FA Youth Cup … ten years on, they were chasing silverware again with United and helping England in their quest for World Cup glory.

Gary Neville

International tournaments have been unkind to the Neville family. Phil Neville was left out of the England World Cup squad in 1998 and in 2002. Phil did play at Euro 2000, but he then became the unlucky scapegoat for England's early knock-out, after giving away a penalty against Romania. In 2002, the bad luck also affected Phil's big brother, Gary Neville.

It was a cruel, cruel blow. After some great performances for United, Gary was a certainty to start at right-back for England in Japan. But then the curse struck – just two weeks before Sven Goran Eriksson named his squad, Gary broke a metatarsal bone in his foot in the Champions League semi-final against Bayer Leverkusen. Funnily enough, his best friend Becks had suffered the same injury, but Gary wasn't laughing. Missing the World Cup Finals and missing out on trophies had taken the gloss off his season.

It had otherwise been another excellent campaign in terms of Gary's progress as an individual player. Before the injury, he started every game for United except four. And out of the four he missed, the Reds lost three! There's no doubt, Gary is one of the country's top defenders, able to switch from right-back to centre-back with ease. In fact, one of United's best spells during 2001/02 came when Gary played alongside Laurent Blanc in the middle, with Phil Neville at right-back and Mikael Silvestre on the left.

It's a stat: Gary earned his 50th cap for England in the 1–1 friendly draw in Holland in February 2002.

Paul Scholes

Paul Scholes had a season of two halves in 2001/02. In the first half, the coaches thought he would be the ideal man to play slightly behind Ruud van Nistelrooy. It's a position some people call "The Hole", others simply "The Teddy Sheringham Position", in honour of the man who used to play there for United and England. Whatever you call it, it didn't work out for Paul – he looked much happier and played much

better when he dropped back into midfield, either in the centre or out on the left.

Paul's personal highlights of 2001/02 all came after Christmas. His match-winning performance against Newcastle at Old Trafford stands out, but he was an even greater threat on the road. Scholes scored in four of the six Premiership away matches that United played in March and April, against Derby (2–2), West Ham (5–3), Leeds (4–3) and Chelsea (3–0).

No wonder Sir Alex Ferguson rates Paul so highly. In spite of his early season problems, Scholes was always one of the first names on the manager's teamsheet – only Laurent Blanc and Fabien Barthez made more appearances than he did in 2001/02. And like Barthez, Paul's involvement in the 2002 World Cup Finals was never in doubt. Sven Goran Eriksson knew early on that Scholes would be one of his star players for England. He just had to pray that, unlike Becks and Gary Neville, Paul wouldn't get injured.

It's a stat: Paul's goal against West Ham at Upton Park on 16 March 2002 was United's 100th of the 2001/02 season.

Nicky Butt

Nicky's hopes of regular first-team football seemed to be seriously threatened by the arrival of Juan Sebastian Veron in 2001. After all, the Argentine superstar had cost the club £28.1 million, considerably more than the cost of developing Nicky from a talented local lad into a top-class midfielder. Pundits predicted that while Veron would slot into a world-class midfield with Giggs, Beckham and Keane, Butt would slip out of Old Trafford and walk into any other Premiership team of his

choice. In truth, it was never going to happen. Sir Alex Ferguson revealed at a press conference in April 2002 that he has never been tempted to sell Nicky, despite receiving more enquiring phone calls about him than about any other player in his time as United boss. Butt's loyalty is priceless. Never one to moan, he comes into the team with the minimum of fuss but often with the maximum effect.

Sir Alex says Nicky was the key to United's revival in the middle of the 2001/02 season, his no-nonsense approach helping to pull the Reds up by their boot-laces. When he started nine matches in a row, from 5 December 2001 to 6 January 2002, United won eight of them. The results were similar when Nicky had an even longer run in the side in March/April, starting with the 5–3 win at West Ham in which he scored with a spectacular overhead kick. Mark Fergie's words, Nicky's here to stay.

It's a stat: Nicky made his 300th appearance for United against Southampton on 22 December 2001.

Far Left : **Neville battles bravely with Varga of Sunderland.**
Left: **Scholes anticipates his next chance.**
Below: **Butt beats Boateng of Villa to the ball.**

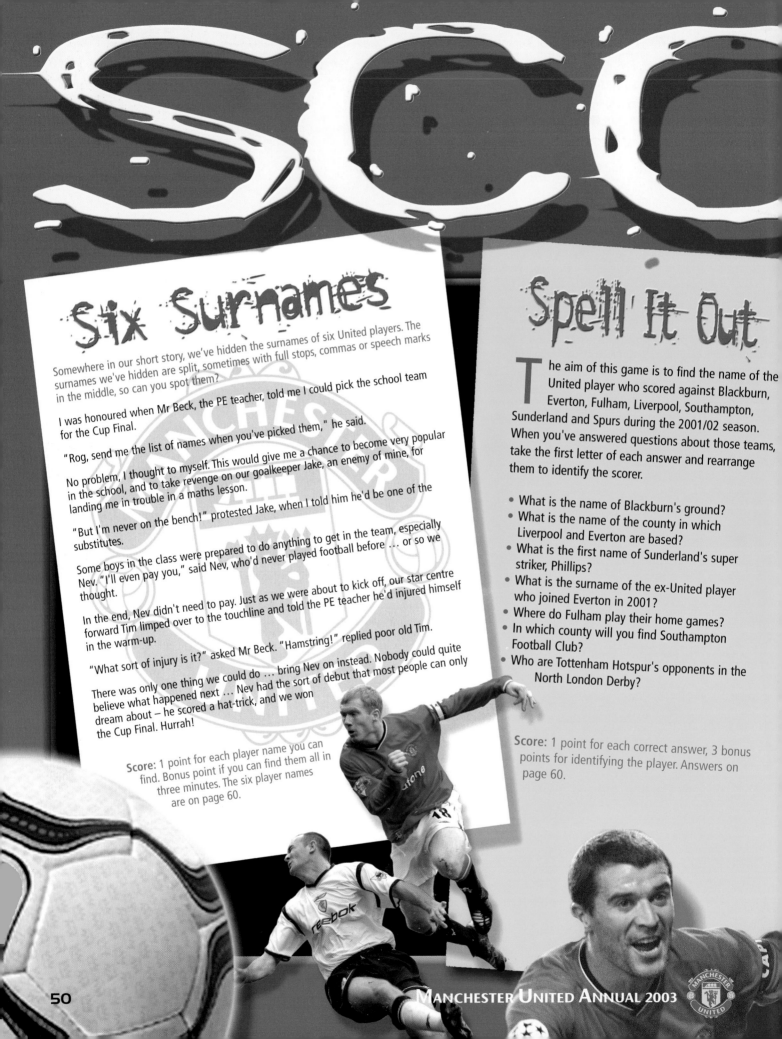

Six Surnames

Somewhere in our short story, we've hidden the surnames of six United players. The surnames we've hidden are split, sometimes with full stops, commas or speech marks in the middle, so can you spot them?

I was honoured when Mr Beck, the PE teacher, told me I could pick the school team for the Cup Final.

"Rog, send me the list of names when you've picked them," he said.

No problem, I thought to myself. This would give me a chance to become very popular in the school, and to take revenge on our goalkeeper Jake, an enemy of mine, for landing me in trouble in a maths lesson.

"But I'm never on the bench!" protested Jake, when I told him he'd be one of the substitutes.

Some boys in the class were prepared to do anything to get in the team, especially Nev. "I'll even pay you," said Nev, who'd never played football before … or so we thought.

In the end, Nev didn't need to pay. Just as we were about to kick off, our star centre forward Tim limped over to the touchline and told the PE teacher he'd injured himself in the warm-up.

"What sort of injury is it?" asked Mr Beck. "Hamstring!" replied poor old Tim.

There was only one thing we could do … bring Nev on instead. Nobody could quite believe what happened next … Nev had the sort of debut that most people can only dream about – he scored a hat-trick, and we won the Cup Final. Hurrah!

Score: 1 point for each player name you can find. Bonus point if you can find them all in three minutes. The six player names are on page 60.

Spell It Out

The aim of this game is to find the name of the United player who scored against Blackburn, Everton, Fulham, Liverpool, Southampton, Sunderland and Spurs during the 2001/02 season. When you've answered questions about those teams, take the first letter of each answer and rearrange them to identify the scorer.

- What is the name of Blackburn's ground?
- What is the name of the county in which Liverpool and Everton are based?
- What is the first name of Sunderland's super striker, Phillips?
- What is the surname of the ex-United player who joined Everton in 2001?
- Where do Fulham play their home games?
- In which county will you find Southampton Football Club?
- Who are Tottenham Hotspur's opponents in the North London Derby?

Score: 1 point for each correct answer, 3 bonus points for identifying the player. Answers on page 60.

Fill In The Blancs

This is our tribute to United's great French defender Laurent Blanc! The object of this game is to make sense of the match report, by replacing the word Blanc with the proper word from the list below. Beware though, some of the words in the list are red herrings…

"United really dominated the Blanc in the first Blanc. In the fifteenth Blanc, Liverpool were just chasing the Blanc as Giggs, Beckham, Scholes and Keane passed it around in Blanc. Then, all of a sudden, the ball was played through to van Nistelrooy, who tested the Liverpool Blanc with a ferocious Blanc from a distance of 25 Blancs. The goalkeeper made a great Blanc, tipping the ball over the Blanc. Beckham took the Blanc on the right-hand side, and found Solskjaer unmarked in the Blanc. The Norwegian made no mistake, scoring his twentieth Blanc of the Blanc. 1–0 to Blanc!"

Select from: goal, half, ball, midfield, shot, minute, yards, crossbar, box, season, save, match, referee, miles, century, bath, photograph, goalkeeper, cliff, United, Stenhousemuir, corner.

Score: 1 point for each word you put in the correct order. The correct order can be found on page 60.

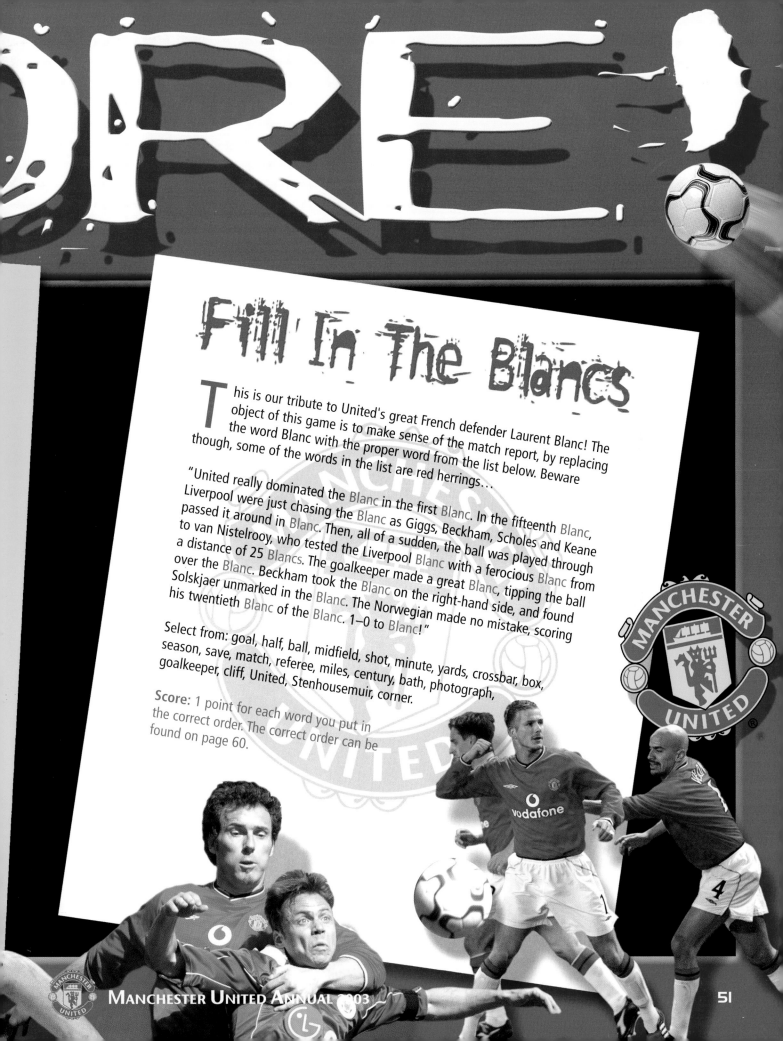

The influence that Manchester United's first French player had on the club and especially the fans will never be forgotten. But five years on from Eric Cantona's early retirement, a trio of men from across the Channel are keeping the Tricolour flag flying high at Old Trafford. Goalkeeper **Fabien Barthez,** centre-back **Laurent Blanc** and left-back **Mikael Silvestre** have done for United's defence what Eric did for the attack, enhancing it with their French flair ...

Fabien Barthez

Fabien Barthez continued to do in his second season at Manchester United what he'd done in his first, by giving his manager, team-mates and supporters some heart-stopping moments of excitement. The difference in 2001/02 was that some of his madcap gambles did not pay off, gifting the opposition goals and points in some important matches.

In fairness to Fabien, the few mistakes that he made were punished by some of Europe's finest forwards, such as Thierry Henry, Michael Owen and Diego Tristan. And they were made at a time when United were having a mini-crisis, their so-called annual blip, in October and November 2001.

When the team turned the corner, Barthez turned it with them and went back to his unbeatable best ... well, almost unbeatable. Opponents managed to sneak the odd goal here and there, but from early December until the end of the season, only

West Ham and Leeds could score more than two against him. Both of those games were away from home, and United won them both, 5–3 and 4–3.

Supporters love scorelines like those, in games that are full of goals and incidents at both ends of the field. Fabien is no different. He likes to entertain, he loves to come off his line, he lives to win in style. If he wanted to win every game 1–0, he'd move to Italy and be bored to tears, no doubt!

It's a stat: Fabien celebrated his 50th appearance for United by keeping a clean sheet in the 4–0 win over Ipswich Town in September 2001.

Laurent Blanc

Laurent Blanc joined Manchester United from Inter Milan in August 2001, not long after Jaap Stam was controversially sold to Lazio. This sudden change of central defender took everyone by surprise, including Stam himself!

Many people, including United's enemies in the media, wondered whether Sir Alex Ferguson had made a big mistake. After all, Blanc was aged 35, while Stam was still approaching the peak of his career. The critics were ready to have a field day, just as soon as Laurent put his first foot wrong.

And it happened. It was bound to. Not even a man who has won the World Cup and European Championships with his country can claim to be the perfect player – but what was disappointing for Laurent was the way in which every error he made seemed to be highlighted by the critics. It didn't help that United's first five league defeats were against Bolton, Liverpool, Arsenal, Newcastle and Chelsea – the first letters of those teams spell out his surname!

Of course, nobody bothered to play word games or write headlines on the countless occasions when Blanc used his excellent reading and tackling skills to shut down opposing attacks. Or when he popped up in the box to score goals against Boavista (home and away) and Tottenham. No, if Laurent needed to receive praise for all the positive things he did in his first season,

he'd turn not to the back pages, but to his appreciative manager. In March 2002, Sir Alex said, "Laurent has proved he is a great, great player. He's the best centre-half I've worked with at this club."

It's a stat: Laurent was France's second-most capped player when he retired from international football with 96 appearances.

Mikael Silvestre

Mikael Silvestre belongs to a different generation of the French national team. While Laurent Blanc is part of its glorious past, Mikael aims to be part of its wonderful future. He picked up his first international winner's medal in the 2001 Confederations Cup in Japan, just a few months after first breaking into the national side ... ironically in Laurent's position, centre-back.

As for his United career, Silvestre has made the left-back position his own after seeing off the challenge from Denis Irwin and, to a lesser extent, from Phil Neville. It wasn't difficult to see why. At times during 2001/02, he was simply outstanding ... for example, in the 2–0 win away to Deportivo La Coruna. In that match, he used his explosive pace to nip several dangerous situations in the bud. Going forward, he set up the second goal for Ruud van Nistelrooy with a low cross into the box. The same combination, earlier in the season, had helped United to draw 1–1 away to Bayern Munich.

Not only can Mikael prevent or create goals, he can also score them. It doesn't happen quite so often, however – his header in the 5–1 win over Nantes last season was only his second for the Reds. Hopefully he can build on that if he continues to make those exciting runs down the left wing.

It's a stat: Mikael made more appearances for United during 2001/02 than any other player.

FERGIE'S FINEST TEAM

Millions of United fans breathed a sigh of relief when **Sir Alex Ferguson** changed his mind about retiring. The great manager has put together some of the greatest teams in the club's long history, from the **1990 FA Cup** side to the **Double Winners of 1994** and the **Treble Winners of 1999**. But what if he could pick players from different years to line up in the same eleven? Would this be his finest ever team?

1 Goalkeeper

Editor's Choice: **Peter Schmeichel**

Your Choice:

It would be very difficult for Sir Alex to decide between Peter Schmeichel, who won the European Championships in 1992, and Fabien Barthez, who won both Euro 2000 and the 1998 World Cup. However, the editor's vote goes to Schmeichel, not only for his greater ability in one-on-one situations but also for saving Dennis Bergkamp's penalty in the last minute of the 1999 FA Cup semi-final replay. That save kept the Treble alive!

Other nominees: **Fabien Barthez, Raimond van der Gouw, Jim Leighton, Les Sealey.**

2 Right-Back

Editor's Choice: **Gary Neville**

Your Choice:

Only a few nominees for this position, partly because Gary Neville has dominated it for so long. He can also play in the middle, but it's mainly at right-back that he's helped United to win Premiership titles, FA Cups and the European Cup. He's also earned lots of caps for England. Others that you might like to consider are Gary's brother Phil, and Denis Irwin, who played on the right when he first joined United.

Other nominees: **Phil Neville, Paul Parker, Denis Irwin.**

3 Left-Back

Editor's Choice: **Denis Irwin**

Your Choice:

No player has been more reliable than Denis Irwin during Fergie's long reign. Never one to make all the headlines or hog the limelight, he has still been one of the manager's most important players. He even took free-kicks and penalties before a kid called David Beckham came along! Everyone was sad to see Denis leave at the end of 2001/02, but at least his old position is now in good hands with Mikael Silvestre.

Other nominees: **Clayton Blackmore, Phil Neville, Mikael Silvestre.**

4 & 5 Centre-Backs

Editor's Choice: **Laurent Blanc & Gary Pallister**

Your Choice:

All successful teams need a solid partnership in the heart of their defence, and United have had some great duos there down the years. For that reason, the editor was tempted to pick the pair of Steve Bruce and Gary Pallister who played together from 1989 to 1996. Jaap Stam and Ronny Johnsen were also considered but in the end the editor couldn't leave out Laurent Blanc. Although he had his critics in his season at United, the Frenchman also had plenty of admirers, including Sir Alex himself, who said: "Laurent Blanc has been the best centre-half I've worked with in my time at this club. He's a fantastic player."

Other nominees: **Henning Berg, Wes Brown, Steve Bruce, Ronny Johnsen, Gary Neville, Jaap Stam.**

6 & 8 Centre Midfield

Editor's Choice: **Roy Keane & Bryan Robson**

Your Choice:

Another part of the team in which you need a terrific twosome is in midfield, in what is sometimes known as the engine room. Like the engine of the car, the people who play in that position provide the power and the energy to drive the team forward. Nobody has done more in this vital area for United in recent years than Roy Keane, while the main man before him was Bryan Robson. He earned the nickname Captain Marvel during his years of winning FA Cups and battling for League Championships.

Other nominees: **Nicky Butt, Paul Ince, Mike Phelan, Paul Scholes, Neil Webb.**

9 Right Midfield

Editor's Choice: **Andrei Kanchelskis**

Your Choice:

Some fans could not imagine a team without David Beckham, whose ability to pass and score from long range has made him one of the world's best midfielders. But those with slightly longer memories will know there was a different type of winger in the team of 1994. Andrei Kanchelskis had electrifying

pace and close control that kept the ball at his feet even when he was making his most rapid raids on the right flank.

Other nominees: **David Beckham, Luke Chadwick.**

11 Left Midfield

Editor's Choice: **Ryan Giggs**

Your Choice:

No disrespect to the other nominees, but nobody can seriously rival Ryan for the left wing position. One or two of the others might have been able to cross the ball just as well if not better, but in terms of running with it and tricking his way past defenders, Giggs is the number one. He's also scored plenty of goals for United, almost 100 in fact. And not just with his left boot, Ryan is also a good header of the ball!

Other nominees: **Jesper Blomqvist, Quinton Fortune, Lee Sharpe.**

7 & 10 Centre Forwards

Editor's Choice: **Eric Cantona & Ruud van Nistelrooy**

Your Choice:

After picking the best back four and keeper to protect your goal, and the most creative midfield to set up your attacks, all you need is to find the best forwards to put the ball in the net. Sir Alex Ferguson would be spoiled for choice if he looked back and tried to pick the best two from all the strikers he has managed. Picking two from four was difficult enough during the Treble season! He then had Andy Cole, Dwight Yorke, Ole Gunnar Solskjaer and Teddy Sheringham in his squad, but even they might struggle to pip our pair ... the genius of 1992 to 1997, Eric Cantona, and the top man of 2001/02, Ruud van Nistelrooy.

Other nominees:
Andy Cole, Mark Hughes, Brian McClair, Teddy Sheringham, Ole Gunnar Solskjaer, Dwight Yorke.

Legendary goalkeeper Peter Schmeichel. Would the Dane be in your dream team?

Champ

If you thought **Manchester United** didn't win anything in 2001/02, you should think again! United Reserves were in fact crowned champions of their league for the first time in five years. It was a great achievement by the young team, coached by ex-United hero Brian McClair …

David Beckham: A shining example of how Reserve Team players can make it to the big time.

Familiar Faces

Reserve team football isn't just for young players on the way up … it's also for senior players making their way back from injury, or for those who need a game to sharpen up their match fitness after weeks of sitting on the first team bench. David May is one example – the experienced defender who played in United's Championship teams of 1996 and 1997 was a key figure for the reserves in 2001/02, making eleven appearances and scoring the goal of the season! Other familiar faces who helped the reserves to win their title include Quinton Fortune, Dwight Yorke, Raimond van der Gouw, Denis Irwin, Wes Brown, Nicky Butt, Phil Neville, Diego Forlan, Ole Gunnar Solskjaer, Andy Cole and Ronny Johnsen.

Michael Stewart: The promising young Scot celebrating with the Reserve League trophy.

Bridging the Gap

Playing for the reserves is an important step on the ladder for any young player dreaming of first team fame and fortune. Once they've outgrown the Academy, where the oldest team is aged Under-19, they move up to join the reserve team that they hope will act as a springboard into the senior squad. Sometimes it happens – David Beckham, Nicky Butt and Paul Scholes all starred for United Reserves before leaping into the big time. Sometimes it doesn't – for one reason or another, a young player might find it too difficult to make the final step from reserves to first team. Eventually they may decide to leave and join a club in a lower division, taking with them an excellent football education and the best wishes of Manchester United's caring coaching staff.

Quinton Fortune: One of the senior stars who helped United Reserves win their title.

Blending Young and Old

The names we've just reeled off would make up a very strong team in the Premiership, let alone in the Reserve League! The rules would have allowed Brian McClair to pick that eleven if he'd wanted to, but that would have done very little to help one of the main aims of the reserve team – to develop young players. The best reserve teams have a blend of young and older players, in which the senior stars play alongside lads in their teens or early twenties and pass on their valuable experience. The partnership in central defence between David May (aged 31) and John O'Shea (21) worked very well – in fact John did so well that he was called up to the first team a few times. Other reserve team regulars who played for United in the Premiership in 2001/02 were the captain Michael Stewart and winger Luke Chadwick.

Award Winners

John O'Shea's impressive progress also earned him a prestigious club award. The United coaching staff named him as the Denzil Haroun Reserve Player of the Year, an honour previously won by players like Nicky Butt (in 1993/94) and Lee Martin (1987/88) who went on to score the winning goal in the 1990 FA Cup final. O'Shea's team-mate, 19-year-old midfielder Paul Tierney, was named the Jimmy Murphy Young Player of the Year after making 19 appearances for the reserves. Previous winners of Paul's award include Ryan Giggs and Wes Brown, who both won the honour twice.

John O'Shea: The impressive Irish defender was named the Reserve Player of the Year.

Choccy's Choice

Brian "Choccy" McClair was delighted when his young team squeezed past the North-East clubs Newcastle, Middlesbrough and Sunderland to win the FA Premier Reserve League.

"It's great for players to win things," Brian told Manchester United magazine. "When I was a player I liked winning the reserve league and as a coach I do as well."

Choccy's success was all the more admirable because it was only his first season on the United coaching staff, following his appointment in July 2001. He'd been away for three years with Motherwell, Blackburn and then taking a break from the game, having left Old Trafford as a player at the end of the 1997/98 season. During his long career as a United player, he won almost every trophy in football, including the Premier League and FA Cup Double in 1994 and 1996 and the Reserve League in 1997 – the last time the Reds won it prior to 2001/02. This valuable experience helped to steer the reserves to their title success in a tense finale to an exciting season.

Did You Know?

All of United Reserves' league matches are shown live and exclusively on MUTV, the club's television channel. If you missed the coverage last season, you missed some great games … such as 7–2 against Bradford, 5–1 against Sheffield Wednesday and 3–2 against Liverpool. **To subscribe to MUTV call 0870 901 0902.**

Championship Form

FA Premier Reserve League Results

2001

Wed 29/8	Middlesbrough (A)	2–2
Thurs 6/9	Sunderland (H)	3–0
Thurs 13/9	Liverpool (H)	3–2
Thurs 18/10	Bradford City (A)	7–2
Thurs 25/10	Aston Villa (H)	1–0
Thurs 1/11	Sheffield Wednesday (H)	5–1
Tues 13/11	Everton (A)	3–1
Thurs 22/11	Man City (H)	1–1
Thurs 6/12	Blackburn Rovers (A)	3–1
Thurs 20/12	Bolton (H)	2–4

2002

Thurs 17/1	Middlesbrough (H)	1–0
Mon 21/1	Sunderland (A)	0–0
Wed 13/2	Bolton (A)	3–0
Thurs 21/2	Aston Villa (A)	0–1
Thurs 28/2	Bradford (H)	1–1
Mon 4/3	Newcastle (A)	2–5
Thurs 14/3	Blackburn Rovers (H)	1–2
Wed 20/3	Liverpool (A)	1–1
Tues 26/3	Sheffield Wednesday (A)	2–0
Thurs 4/4	Newcastle (H)	0–0
Tue 9/4	Man City (A)	1–1
Thurs 18/4	Everton (H)	2–1
Thurs 25/4	Leeds (A)	2–0
Mon 6/5	Leeds (H)	1–2

FA Premier Reserve League (North)

Top Six (Final)	P	W	D	L	F	A	Pts
Manchester Utd	24	12	7	5	47	28	43
Newcastle Utd	24	13	3	7	46	27	42
Middlesbrough	24	12	6	6	36	26	42
Sunderland	24	12	4	8	43	28	40
Bolton Wanderers	24	12	3	9	45	40	39
Manchester City	24	10	7	7	40	28	37

FRED THE RED AND THE TRAINING RUN

PRE-SEASON TRAINING HAS JUST STARTED, AND SIR ALEX AND THE COACHING STAFF WANT TO GET THE TEAM BACK TO MATCH FITNESS AFTER THE SUMMER HOLIDAYS. TODAY THEY'VE ORGANISED A CROSS COUNTRY RUN DOWN BY THE COAST...

OK, LADS! YOU RUN DOWN THE CLIFF PATH TO THE BEACH, THEN ACROSS THE SAND DUNES TO THE END OF THE BAY. THEN BACK UP THE CLIFF AND THROUGH THE WOODS. FINALLY BACK TO THE VILLAGE. IT'S ABOUT 10 MILES...

RACE YOU!

BET I'M FIRST!!

I HATE CROSS COUNTRY RUNS. I'M ALWAYS LAST!

THE SQUAD SPEEDS OFF...

PUFF!

AT THE SAND-DUNES...

PHEW! I'M LOST. I WISH I'D LISTENED A BIT HARDER TO THE DIRECTIONS...

Answers to Puzzles

Extra Time
(page 29)

Set 1
1. Portugal
2. Deportivo La Coruna
3. Eight (1–2, 2–3, 2–0, 3–2)
4. Mickael Landreau
5. Two – Bayer Leverkusen and Bayern Munich
6. Olympiakos Piraeus

Set 2
1. Eric Cantona
2. Leeds United, Blackburn Rovers, Arsenal
3. Four – 1993, 1994, 1996 and 1997
4. Blackburn Rovers
5. Jesper Blomqvist, Jaap Stam, Dwight Yorke
6. Henning Berg, Ronny Johnsen, Erik Nevland, Ole Gunnar Solskjaer

Set 3
1. East
2. West
3. South
4. North
5. East and South
6. North

Set 4
1. Villa Park
2. He'd scored in eight Premier League games in a row.
3. Paul Scholes had kicked it into the crowd.
4. United won 2–0, Solskjaer scored both goals.
5. Andy Cole
6. It was his first goal for United.

Set 5
1. England – he went to school in Salford.
2. Roy Carroll
3. Michael Stewart
4. Giggs and Veron (Wales played Argentina in a friendly.)
5. Greece and Sweden
6. Quinton Fortune

Set 6
1. Rangers
2. Cathy
3. Darren
4. Horse racing
5. November 1986
6. The FA Cup in 1990

Can You Win the Treble? Ratings (pages 16–17)

Squares 1–21: Very poor, the trophy cupboard is bare! Have a look at the last match square you passed or landed on, to see which round you managed to get to in the FA Cup.

Squares 20–40: Very good, you won the FA Cup but missed out on the Premier League! Have a look at the match squares between your final square and square 42, to see which teams finished above you.

Squares 41–59: Excellent, you won the Premier League and the FA Cup, but fell short in Europe. Have a look at the last match square you passed or landed on, to see which round you reached in the European Cup.

Square 60: Fantastic! You won the Treble of Premier League, FA Cup and European Cup. Expect a call to Buckingham Palace to receive your knighthood. Well done, Sir!

South American Idols

Question at end of page 35:

The twelve nations are:
Argentina (Veron)
Australia (Bosnich)
Czech Republic (Poborsky)
Denmark (Olsen, Sivebaek, Schmeichel)
France (Barthez, Blanc, Cantona, Prunier, Silvestre)
Holland (Cruyff, Stam, Van der Gouw, Van Nistelrooy)
Italy (Taibi)
Norway (Berg, Johnsen, Nevland, Solskjaer)
South Africa (Fortune)
Sweden (Blomqvist)
Ukraine (Kanchelskis)
Yugoslavia (Jovanovic)

Score!
(pages 50–51)

Six Surnames
1. **Keane:** our goalkeeper Jake, an enemy of mine
2. **Forlan:** for landing me in trouble
3. **Veron:** But I'm never on the bench!
4. **Neville:** especially Nev. "I'll even pay you,"
5. **Beckham:** asked Mr Beck. "Hamstring!"
6. **Butt:** the sort of debut that most people

Spell It Out
1. Ewood Park
2. Merseyside
3. Kevin
4. Blomqvist
5. Craven Cottage
6. Hampshire
7. Arsenal
Player's name: Beckham

Fill in the Blancs
Correct order of words: match, half, minute, ball, midfield, goalkeeper, shot, yards, save, crossbar, corner, box, goal, season, United.

Who's Who?

If you're having trouble making out the autographs on the inside front and back covers, here's some help. How many did you get right?

David Beckham
Fabien Barthez
Juan Sebastian Veron
Mikael Silvestre
Paul Scholes
Nicky Butt
Ole Gunnar Solskjaer

Phil Neville
Quinton Fortune
Diego Forlan
Roy Keane
Wes Brown
Ruud van Nistelrooy
Ryan Giggs
Gary Neville

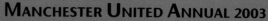